Edgar Fawcett

Fabian Dimitry

A Novel

Edgar Fawcett

Fabian Dimitry
A Novel

ISBN/EAN: 9783337026349

Printed in Europe, USA, Canada, Australia, Japan

Cover: Foto ©Thomas Meinert / pixelio.de

More available books at **www.hansebooks.com**

The Rialto Series.   Vol. 1, No. 25.   May, 1890.   Monthly.   Subscription $8.00 a year.
Entered as second-class matter at the Post Office, Chicago, Ill., Feb. 16, 1889.

Fabian Dimitry.

BY

EDGAR

FAWCETT.

RAND, McNALLY & COMPANY,

CHICAGO AND NEW YORK.

FABIAN DIMITRY.

FABIAN DIMITRY

A Novel

BY

EDGAR FAWCETT,

AUTHOR OF

"THE EVIL THAT MEN DO," "OLIVIA DELAPLAINE," ETC.

———

CHICAGO AND NEW YORK:

RAND, MCNALLY & COMPANY, PUBLISHERS.

1890.

TO LILIAN WHITING,

IN APPRECIATION OF HER NOBLE AND WOMANLY

INTELLECT, HER LOFTY IDEALS,

AND HER VALUED ENCOURAGEMENTS.

New York, January, 1896.

FABIAN DIMITRY.

I.

Who has not seen the multicolored lights
of the Alhambra flame in Leicester Square
from the gloom of a London evening? Almost
every third American whom one meets, it
might now be answered, in these days when
the awful sweep of ocean from New York to
Liverpool has become like the trivial terrors
of a swollen brook. Still, by early November,
there are few transatlantic theatre-goers
remaining in "the gray metropolis of the
North." Either they have all sped home
again across those heaving marine leagues
which they contemn so magnificently, or they
have drifted to the south of Europe in
search of that clement thermometer which
they rarely find above the toe of the Italian
boot.

Ray Eninger, though an American, had
not migrated from London at all, much as
he detested tawny fogs and vacillant rain-
spirts.   He had found himself in the region
of Piccadilly at about nine o'clock, and had
half made up his mind to seek a book and
a hearth-blaze at his easeful Jermyn Street
lodgings.   But great vapors that had hid
the sun all day had now rolled from a sky
full of soft yet keen stars, whose silver peace
mocked the turbulence below them.   Eninger
had passed the glare of the Criterion and the
Pavilion with a sense of gaining some sort of
real repose both for eye and ear a little
further on.   But though Leicester Square
was in a way quieter, with its lines of drowsy
cabs and its heavy central masses of shadow,
the two huge luminiferous theatres which
presently rose before him were but aggressive
repetitions of the structures he had already
left behind him.   The Empire he had always
thought peculiarly and Britishly vulgar.   The
Alhambra he had not visited in several years,
and a caprice to do so here assailed him
with such an unforeseen suddenness that he

indolently yielded to it. He had no sooner
strolled past its radiant portals, however, than
he became the prey of a bored feeling. "England is a man's country," somebody had
said to him not long ago, and he had never
more clearly seen the truth of this bold
phrase than just here and now. The women
present were presumably not all of a lax
trend. Some were, as a glance at them told
you while you observed them strolling unes-
corted through the arabesqued and sumptuous lobbies; but others had not their brassy
stamp, and might, for all one knew, be
seated beside their true lords with whom
they had come hither from chaste homes in
Brompton or Chelsea. And yet the men
ungallantly clouded the air with smoke, or
drank from little shelf-like stands in front
of them the potions of clubs and taverns.
It was a splendid, even a patrician interior.
Its immensity invited the roving eye, which
lit on nothing tawdry, on much that was
artistic. The ballet then in course of prog-
ress might have shamed our own Niblo's
Garden at its finest. It seemed as if the

stage could hold no more of spectacular and
processional pomp, whereupon new lanes of
light would burn among its amazons and bac-
chantes as new phalanxes of bright-clad
shapes came marching from viewless lairs.
The entire scale of the entertainment was
so fine and distinguished, in spite of its
commonness as mere drama, that Eninger
asked himself why drink and tobacco should
be permitted thus to flout and cheapen its
handsome smartness. He had bought a
stall but did not choose to take it. He kept
wandering hither and thither, with half a
mind to drop in rumination on one of the
velvet lounges and half a mind to wander
forth again below the inconstant London
stars. People passed and repassed him, but
he scarcely noted their faces, irritated with
himself for having let his feet stroll where
all men and women must of necessity be
strangers. He was a man marked among
his friends for an excessive nicety and fas-
tidiousness. He had been called, both in
New York and London, a snob, yet unjustly
when all was said. The Alhambra now

emphasized for him a rawness of life from which he shrank and had always shrunk. Possessed of a fairly generous income, having chosen the career of a physician from desire rather than need, being endowed with a tall, trim shape and a visage blond, delicate though virile, equipped with a charm of tactful mien and talk not usual among men of even the older races, he had shone a kind of social star in circles where he had not sought to push entrance yet whose reigning powers had welcomed him on terms of peculiar flattery and acclaim. Not long ago, at one of the great English country-houses, he had committed what now remorsefully pierced him as an act of dismal folly. A certain Lady Beatrice Brashleigh, daughter of an earl and niece of a duke, had won him, with the blue of her big eyes and the music of her suave voice, into an avowal of passion. Lady Beatrice did not, by any means, fix a vacant stare on the presumptuous American or endeavor to slay him with her noble birth. She simply burst into tears and murmured something about papa objecting; and soon

Eninger had found out that papa did seriously object. His transatlantic origin was not
a chief drawback to the match, for the earl
was by no means a rich peer and Lady Beatrice had a bevy of sisters. But for an American suitor Eninger·could not make meaning
enough settlements. Such a marriage as that,
declared his lordship, must have a heavy
golden reason for being. In the case of Eninger it was golden, but not sufficiently heavy.

He left Brashleigh House one misty Sep-
tember morning, and fancied that as he cast
an upward look at its ivied stonework he
caught one vague glimpse of a maiden's pale
and tear-stained face. But the vision did not
haunt him long. What haunted him much
longer was the cut, the sting that had been
dealt his pride. He had, after all, been in
love with Lady Beatrice more through
imagination than heart. He had liked that
historic perfume which hovered about her
surroundings with so much of the delightful
tenacity of tradition. Still, he now recalled
his past acquaintance with her rather in the
light of an escape than a sorrow.

"I shouldn't have known what to do with her after I'd got her," he had mused. "Sooner or later I mean hard work as a physician, and New York shall no doubt be the scene of my labors. How absurd it would have looked over there, that 'Dr. and Lady Beatrice Eninger!' And yet she might have clung to her title always, for she was proud of it though ever so fond of me."

For some time, this evening, Eninger sat on one of the velvet lounges and watched, at either of the large buffets which his vision was able to command, that extraordinary capacity of the English theatre-goer for pouring down fiery fluids. The first impression of respectful novelty which even the average Londoner can produce in his kinsman over-sea had long ago lost its force with Eninger. He was used to all the different "types," of whichever sex, and extremely fatigued with most of them. "How peculiarly and specially vulgar," he caught himself thinking, "a vulgar London crowd is able to appear!" . . and then, in a flash of discovery, he saw the man who of all others living he

would have held too refined and fastidious
to pass the lintels of a place like this.

"Why, Fabian!" he exclaimed, and
sprang up from his seat, seizing the arm of
the stroller. Then, as a smile of recognition
answered him, he went on with vehemence:
"What on earth brings *you* here!"

"Do you mean to England, my dear
Ray!" replied the other, with a voice
exquisitely soft and yet somehow not of the
quality one would call womanish. He had,
however, limpid brown eyes which many a
woman might have envied him, and round
his pure-cut, beardless lips lingered the
double spell of sweetness and intellectuality.

Eninger slipped a hand within his friend's
arm. "Oh, I meant," he said, "this great,
smart, beastly place. Come and sit down
for a minute." He turned to look after his
former seat but perceived that it was occu-
pied. He soon glimpsed a distant table,
however, and drew his friend toward it with
an insistent warmth which bore odd contrast
to his former languor. The table was small,
and as they sat down beside it he resumed

merrily: "Let's drink something. Everybody is drinking something, I observe. And
a cigarette—you'll like these, I think;
they're a trifle rare. So the ballet lured
you? Well, it *is* good, what I've seen of it.
Why under heavens didn't I know you were
in London, Fabian? Have you been here a
long time?"

"Nearly a year."

"Nearly a year!" echoed Eninger. "Fancy!" he pursued, unconscious, no doubt,
of the anglicism. "This town is such a
monstrous maze, isn't it? Twin brothers
could live here for an age within the
throw of a stone from one another, and
yet never meet."

"Quite true," acceded Fabian.

"And the last time we met was about two
years ago at one of those semi-literary evening pow-wows which they give so badly in
New York."

"Yes; I remember."

Eninger glanced at him sharply. "My
dear Fabian," he said, "you're not like your
old self."

Fabian smiled, and his face, beautiful and poetic without a smile, drew, when thus illumined, a soft, pleased cry from his companion.

"Ah, that's more like you!" exclaimed Eninger. Then, as the smile faded, he went on: "You once had such glorious spirits. What's tamed them—or who?"

"Who?" repeated Fabian, while he drooped the brown eyes, dark-lashed and lucid, that burned from his oval face.

"Does my interrogative pronoun bore you?" said Eninger; and he lifted to his lips the glass which a waiter had just filled for him. "I do hope you haven't forgotten, dear boy, what tremendous chums we once were at Harvard."

"Indeed I haven't, Ray!"

They looked at one another in silence for a little space. "You're going to account for yourself," announced Eninger, terminating the odd pause. "You're going to tell me something."

"Well, perhaps."

"We ought to have written one another,

Fabian. It's been a horrid shame that we've drifted out of our nice fraternal habit of correspondence. Probably the fault was mine —but no matter whose it was. If we *had* exchanged letters through all these months I might—well, I might have given you an appreciable plot for one of your plays. Or have you renounced the making of plays altogether?"

Fabian slowly shook his head, with what struck Eninger as a subtle melancholy in the motion. "No, Ray, not quite; I suppose I shall always go on groping a little along that line. It's all I ever *could* do, you know."

"But for the present you've neglected your talent?"

"Yes . . And so you've been living through a drama that you think my poor languid muse would care for?"

Eninger gave a curt, ambiguous nod. "I'm not just sure of that," he returned. "My drama is of the Robertsonian school— plenty of small talk, a little satire, and enough comedy to hide the real tragedy of tears behind it. I've no doubt you'd think

2

it very flat and stale. But unless I'm wholly
wrong, Fabian, my opinion of yours would
be ever so different."

Fabian sat staring for some time at the
glass whose contents he had scarcely tasted.
At last he gave a slight start which made his
slender and supple frame actively vibrate.
"Let's get out into the streets," he said,
rising. "We can talk better there. You
evidently think I've been having an infernal
sort of experience, Ray. Does my face tell
you so?"

"By no means," replied Eninger, now rising also. "But it hints to me that you're a
sadder man than when I knew you last."

"Yes—and in some ways a wiser one,"
muttered Fabian, below his breath, while
they quitted the noisy, smoky, brilliant
theatre.

"Which way shall we go?" he added,
after they had gained the refreshing dusk
and coolness of Leicester Square.

"Whatever way you please," Eninger
answered, and soon he forgot all thought of
locality, his friend spoke to him so fluently,

so feverishly, and yet with such a potent charm.

"We're here, almost at her very door," Fabian finally said, after they had pushed their way through a narrow street into a square whose drowsy old trees were murmurous below a late-risen fragment of moon. "Ah, Ray, think of the dramas that a fellow like me could find hidden away among these grim, ancient houses! How still they all are —it's the reticence of death, yet of recollection, too! Yonder's the house where *she* lives. Seven or eight generations of them have lived and died in it. They're poor, now, as I told you. They wouldn't be spending their days in even so fascinatingly picturesque a spot as this Lincoln's Inn Square if poverty hadn't held them here."

"And yet," said Eninger, feeling the need of some sort of speech, "you tell me that you met her with her father summer before last off in the Engadine."

"Oh, yes. The old Colonel's bronchitis had got devilish during the raw spring. They scraped up enough money to take the

trip. You see, there are only two of them,
father and daughter; they can graze starvation without tumbling into it. Still, there's
a big mortgage on that little house, and some
day the very worst may happen. It's hard,
Ray, they're as good blood as any in England, but the last of an impoverished line.
I doubt if half the grandees (some with
titles bought ten years ago) are even aware
they exist."

Eninger stared into his friend's face, which
the glamour of moonlight seemed now to
invest with a new repose, patience and
spirituality. "Alicia Delamere," he said;
"it's a lovely name, certainly. And you say
that she——" Here he broke short off.
"For God's sake, Fabian," he quickly went
on, "why don't you marry her and make an
end of it?"

The sculptural lips of Fabian tightened
together a little. "I've told you why," he
said.

Those words had for his hearer a horrible
pathos and solemnity. "But she loves
you," he began, "and——"

"I think she loves me—yes, I feel inwardly certain of it," struck in Fabian.

"And you love her?"

"Devotedly."

"Then cast that scruple of yours to the winds!" exclaimed Eninger.

"Would *you*, in my place?" queried Fabian, grasping his arm.

"Would I!" he repeated, staggered by the question, as applied to himself. "But I've never seen her—I don't love her."

"If you *did* love her," persisted Fabian, with eyes unrelenting, and with hand that did not in the least relax.

"But I've never loved in that way,", returned Eninger, with an evasive air that was perhaps more apparent because he strove to hide it.

"Ah," said Fabian, dropping his arm, yet slipping an arm of his own round Eninger's neck: "I see that you would have just my torturing hesitancy, were you situated as I."

Together the two friends quitted the moon-lit square, which was for one of them clad evermore in a new spell of gloom and wist-

fulness. Its gray memorials of how men
fade and inanimate things remain, had
always for Eninger been pregnant with sug-
gestion; but now, at this mysterious moment,
not far from midnight, and under this eerie
moon of a London autumn, the whole quarter
(for reasons that chiefly concerned his companion's late discourse) appeared haunted
by the influence of some grisly curse.

II.

Nor did Eninger by any means rid himself of that sensation when he paid, with Fabian, a visit to the Delameres on the following day. The small house in Lincoln's Inn Square was no less shabby within than grimy without, but Alicia Delamere lighted its dinginess as a buttercup lights a dingle. She had hair almost as golden as that flower, and so white a throat that it made the ardent yet velvety blue of her eyes burn all the more deliciously keen. Her figure, however, as Eninger soon told himself, was by no means a perfection of moulding, although lissome and graceful, while her deportment betokened neither the *air de race* nor the simple equipments of ordinary tact and finish. Watching her with the cold eye of criticism, he pronounced her manners almost piteously deficient. She had pretty hands, but was forever moving them about, like an embar-

rassed child; she would smile naturally one
minute and artificially the next; her post-
ures, whether she sat or stood, were one
perpetual bashful unrest. And yet it soon
began to dawn upon Eninger that she was
irresistibly charming. It was not that he
grew to approve her, but rather that he took
a secret pleasure in watching her defects.
She was not at all like an English girl, nor
yet like an American : she had far too little
gravity for the first and far too much reserve
for the last. Eninger got rapidly to be fond
of watching her; she made him think of a
briar-rose in a breeze, of a little ruffled
brook between fringes of cresses. Her wild-
ing sort of demureness refreshed him after
the correct repose of Lady Beatrice. Then,
too, there was a pathos in her shyness. For
had not Fabian told him that her mother had
died when the dug was at her baby lip, and
did not this gaunt, sour old spectre of a
father look as though he could no more rear
a delicate young daughter than stand on his
bullet-shaped, grizzled head?

It struck the new-comer as the head of a

possibly stupid man, and he soon learned
that he had rightly judged it. But Colonel
Delamere was not simply stupid. He at
once fixed a fishy, viscous eye on Eninger,
and paid him all the court that his absurdly stiff deportment permitted him to
proffer. He was a man who in earlier life
had been very arrogant, and after the fashion
of arrogance that we sometimes may see full-
blown in the military Englishman. He had
never known just how to bend his back, even
when the iron goad of penury smote it—
though indeed there had been a good deal of
bending with him, as many knew. But
after Eninger had become, during the next
fortnight or so, a confirmed visitor at his dismal old domicile, he showed signs of soci-
ality, rare with him as imprudence in a
weasel.

Meanwhile, on one or two occasions, Fabian was surprised at finding his friend in the
company of either Alicia or her father. His
surprise quickly wore off, however; for had
he not made a kind of tacit agreement with
Eninger that the latter should observe the

almost unique dolor of his own situation? Not that Fabian looked for any help from his friend's future counsels. Alas! he had more than once meditated, how could there be any earthly help away from the fulfillment of what he held inexorable duty? The path was all too frightfully plain; Ray Eninger could make it neither more nor less so!

One evening he dropped into the latter's Jermyn Street apartments, with a rueful white on his cheeks and a glassy feverishness in his splendid brown eyes. "Did you not tell me, a day or two ago. Ray." he presently asked, "that you would soon sail for New York?"

Eninger slightly started. "I— I don't remem ——" he began, and then gave a sudden acquiescent nod. "Oh, yes;" he proceeded, "I believe I did say so—carelessly, that is."

Fabian, whose eyes had sought the floor, looked swiftly up at him. "Oh," he said, "then you didn't mean it?" His friend made no answer. and he went on: "I'm sorry."

"Sorry?" repeated Eninger.

"Yes; I wanted to sail with you. I thought
of the *Bolivia* next Saturday."

"So soon as that!" faltered Eninger. He
had turned pale, but hoped that the ruddy
fire-shine, near which he sat in slippers and
dressing-sacque, would guard his altered
hue.

"Why do you call it soon?" murmured
Fabian. "I supposed," he added, sombrely,
"that after all I have told you it would
strike you as late."

Eninger watched the crackling fire. "This
is decisive, then," he said. "You're going
to give her up?"

"Ah, Ray," cried his companion, "haven't
you been sure all along that I meant to do
so?"

"No. I thought——" and there Eninger
paused, still watching the fire.

Fabian rose and took a seat at the side of
his friend. He was tranquil, and yet he
seemed somehow inwardly to tremble.

"Ray," he began, "I have looked for the
last time into the face of these bitter facts.
There is no avoiding their moral meaning to

a man fashioned like myself. If I married
Alicia Delamere, I would be perpetuating a
curse."

Here Eninger made a gesture which his
observer may wrongly have read, for Fabian,
even while he noted it, stoutly pursued:

"Yes, a curse! You know that, Ray—
you must know it, and feel it as I. We're
neither of us believers, as the trick of the
phrase goes. We're not religionists; we don't
do right with a sense of pay to come after
the grave's got us into its dark maw. But
even if death end all for the individual we
accept the claim life exacts while it lasts.
Here is this Delamere race—you know the
stain on it; I told you. None of their own
making, but a stain I can reproduce and
brand my children with if I will. Her father
is the only one of five brothers that was
spared. All the rest were unsound in some
mental way. He has an uncle who's living
still, an idiot, in one of the county asylums.
His own father cut his throat, off in Devon-
shire, one night, after fifty delirious fits and
a kind of three years' calmness that made

people think he would draw his last breath
sane. Yet worse than this, *her* three brothers—and one but a mere lad of twelve—all
perished in tragic manners from the same
hideous ill . . . I've told you this before—
yes, your silence seems to answer me that
I've told it before. But " (and here Fabian
leaned close to his hearer, with a hand on
the back of his chair) " you've something
now in your silence that wasn't there then.
I can read it, though I don't understand it.
Ray, my friend, you can't mean that you
advise me—you, always so finely furnished
with the hate of weak and small acts—*not* to
recoil from this piece of terrible egotism."

Affection and reproach were blended in
Fabian's voice. As Eninger turned and met
his eyes, the result was an electric conscience-
thrill.

"You say that I hate weak and small
acts," he said. "But I can't call this one
of either. It's only human. Good God!
we're not to be bred, we men and women
with minds and souls, as though we were
race-horses!"

"But we're to think of our unborn children. Ray! I've always said that no man had the right to marry a woman with the seeds of an incurable hereditary malady in her blood. We call murder a crime. In begetting the heirs of murderous ills we are ourselves worse than assassins. The selfishness of it all is supreme; we may be laying desolate a score of lives merely to please our own. The bigot, the pietist, the shallow conservative may have his excuse for such a course. Men like you and me, Ray—men who have stamped all superstition underfoot and accepted science as the one help and hope of humanity—we have none!"

Eninger got up from his chair and stood with his back to the fire and with hands clasped behind him. His purplish silken dressing-sacque gave to him a new air of patrician daintiness and nicety. There are men who can not draw on a pair of gloves without implying some peculiar refinement by the process. Eninger was one of these. You had but to watch a little while before you became aware that his tastes and temperament were

porcelain beside the common earthenware of
others. Yet although he clearly bespoke
the dilettant, he never deserved the name of
prig or *poseur*. Certain crudities in his fel-
low-men shocked him past speech, and rather
than dwell under the ban of particular social
conditions he would have courted death.
Shame or disgrace of any sort would have
been like barbed and poisoned darts to him.
His standing before the world, the point of
view that people had of him, the whiteness
and brightness with which his good-name
shone before their eyes, he held surpassingly
dear. As dear, too, was immunity from the
prying public gaze. He had talent enough
to have written something if he had tried;
but the idea of having the newspapers direct
upon his work their calcium glare was
fraught for him with an especial disrelish.
Of all human creatures he was one least
fitted for what we call the battle of life. It
was not simply that the hard knocks he
must get there would give him pain, but
that they dealt him unhealing, immedicable
wounds. And yet he was a man who had

delighted, notwithstanding all this over-refinement and sensitiveness, in confronting many of those austere nineteenth-century truths which have sent romance whimpering and shivering from her ancient coignes and bournes.

In this respect he was mentally akin to his friend, Fabian Dimitry, as we have but recently heard the latter say. But Fabian's organism was of far stouter and manfuller make. On leaving college he had found himself, like Eninger, lifted above the needs of money-getting, though with an income which extravagance might easily have melted. The idea of sending some new red blood into the shrivelled veins of our dramatic literature had thralled and fascinated him. Going abroad, he had studied the stage in several great European cities, and at last had drifted to London deep in the spell of Miss Delamere's attractions. His resolute artistic purpose had remained firm enough until the dawn of a most bewildering trouble. But even now you had only to mark the clear, strong lines of his classic face to see that he

was one whom sorrow might martyrize but
never unman. There was no daintiness nor
over-sensitiveness here. A fine serenity of
spirit controlled this nature, a patient dignity upbore it, and a lucid liberalism sentinelled, so to speak, its approaches.

"You speak of excuses," Eninger slowly
said. "To my thinking there could be only
one that was powerful enough—Alicia Delamere herself."

Fabian gave a start, and then his lips mel-
lowed into a warm smile "You think her
so lovely!" he exclaimed.

Eninger was glancing down at his own delicate white hands, with their filbert nails
like glossy little pink shells and their single
ring, an almost priceless cameo which he
had picked up somewhere in Italy as a really
wondrous *trouraille*. He had often lightly
said, until he chanced upon this gem, that
he would as soon wear a ring through his
nose as one upon his finger.

"I think her a very beautiful creature,"
he now answered. Then he looked up in a
keen, alert way at his friend. "About these

stories of madness being so rampant in the family . . May they not have been exaggerated?"

"No," said Fabian, with a sort of unwilling firmness. "I have made quite sure. The complete record has reached me through sources there was no distrusting. Some other time I'll tell you more. There are ghastly details about those dead Delameres which to-night, Heaven help me, I've no stomach for."

"And the old Colonel?" asked Eninger, in an absent, brooding voice. "Has he volunteered no confidences?"

"None. Poor old fellow, I imagine he thinks Alicia has told me nothing."

"Then his daughter knows and is willing to talk of it all?"

"She knows, but refers to it only with the greatest reluctance. I mean," added Fabian, "when *I* bring up the subject. With you— with any ordinary acquaintance—she would be apt, I think, to decline all discussion of it."

"Ah," said Eninger dryly, perhaps not knowing that he spoke.

Those words "ordinary acquaintance"
jarred upon him. When he thought of the
sudden yet novel emotions roused in him by
Alicia it seemed as if his acquaintance with
her had already become very extraordinary
indeed. Fabian now went on to say that he
had found the old Colonel rather difficult to
get along with. "The truth is," he declared,
with abrupt frankness, "I pity but don't at
all admire him. He's not worthy to be the
father of so dear a girl. His poverty stirs
my compassion, but his lack of dignity
wakes my disgust. Perhaps dignity's too
mild a word, and I ought to call it conscience.
The old sinner borrows of every man who
will lend him, Ray, and with no more idea
of returning the money than if it had been
left him as a legacy. He's the horror of his
club and the despair of his poor child.
Your turn will come soon, if you make many
more visits to Lincoln's Inn Square. Still,
for all I know, it may have come already?"

"It hasn't," said Eninger. He afterward
thought, with an inward shudder, of Alicia's
position. A father like that, besides an

ancestry so forlornly besmirched! How tyrannous were the whims and freaks of destiny! What a mercy if some man were to fling her a stout little plank of matrimony amid these tossing waters of dismay and threat!

After what Fabian had told him about the Colonel, he was prepared to be asked for at least five pounds the next time he and Alicia's father were alone together. But on this occasion (one which arrived much sooner than he had expected) no such request left the grim old soldier's lips. On the contrary a good many rather grumbling remarks left them with respect to the absent Fabian.

"Between ourselves, now, my dear Mr. Eninger," said the Colonel, in his stiff, graceless way, "it strikes me that Dimitry is a devil of a self-assuming person. By Jove, he talks of the drama of this country as though it were all worthless rubbish, right from Shakespeare down."

"Oh, I think he draws the line at Shakespeare," smiled Eninger, who loathed most of the current English play-writing as cor-

dially as his friend did, and knew well how
Fabian loved the divine William.

"No," maintained the Colonel, crossing
his thin legs obstinately, "I'm deuced if he
draws the line anywhere. And what has he
himself done, I'd like to know, in the dramatic line? Plays in manuscript mean nothing till they're produced. You'll grant that!"
continued the Colonel, as if he had suddenly
turned up some shining jewel of wisdom
with the plowshare of everyday discourse.

But he had several more ill-natured things
to say of Fabian, as Eninger soon discovered.
None of his back-biting was more serious
than that of a spleenful old man who fumes
with a grudge. When he began to draw
between Eninger and his friend, however, a
comparison highly flattering to the former,
then light broke upon the Colonel's listener.
"He's ambling gently toward a requested loan
of five pounds," thought Eninger, and he
thought also of Alicia who was off on some
shopping expedition (Heaven only knew if it
were not to haggle with some cheap butcher
about the cutlet's for that evening's dinner,

poor girl!) and told himself that just another
sight of those morning-colored eyes and that
field-daisy sort of face would be worth twice,
even thrice, the sum.

But he had entirely misinterpreted the
sly old Colonel. No attempt was made to
borrow a farthing. In awkward, infelici-
tous fashion he was told that he possessed
points of marked superiority over Fabian
and that this opinion was one which Alicia
also held. Eninger felt his heart throb
as he heard those tidings. It never occurred to him that he was perchance a matri-
monial bait at which were now being given
two or three discreet preliminary nibbles.
Alicia soon appeared, and the Colonel won
his gratitude by rather promptly leaving.
How her eyes lit the room! How her rest-
ive, nervous manner made one long to lull
and pacify her as one might stroke the
fur of a kitten! It must be that she was
forever worrying about their household
debts and her father's reckless borrowings
and the horrid no-thoroughfare prospect of
their future.

As they now sat together near a window that gave upon the square and watched the dismantled trees quiver in a rainy wind beneath low-stooping leaden skies, Eninger had a sense of quiet delight he had never known before. Presently the rain ceased and the sun tried to struggle out from the monstrous masses of rolling vapor that whitened and glistened with his fitful rays. If nowhere in the world there are gloomier heavens than over London, nowhere, too, are there more gloriously mutable and poetic ones, and never an autumn passes but the miraculous canvases of Turner are hundreds of times reduplicated in those azure fields whence he first drew their splendors.

Eninger scarcely knew what he and Alicia talked about that afternoon. The most trifling matters, no doubt, and yet every fresh word seemed to make him feel more intimately at home in her presence. She was so much easier to talk with than most of the English girls whom he had met. They would sit sedately with hands crossed in their laps and expect not to amuse but

to be amused. With Alicia it was not thus;
she thought of pretty, diverting little things
to say; she was cleverer, more buoyant, less
restrained and self-effaced than multitudes
of her English sisters. Eninger at length
tried to learn something of her real feelings
toward Fabian.

"You've known him a good while now,
have you not?" he said.

"Yes; rather." She drooped her eyes.
"But he doesn't come to us as often as he
once did. I can't think why." Here she
raised her eyes again. "Can you?"

"No; unless it's because he is busy thinking out his dramas."

She clasped her hands together and leaned
eagerly forward, while he saw a keener pink
float up into her cheek. "Oh, are they
not strong and fine, those dramas!" she
exclaimed. "He has read me two, 'Rosa-
mond' and 'Married Women.' How different they are from the trash one sees when
one goes to the play here in London. What
warm humanity is in them, yet what sting-
ing satire. And how they take hold of

the mind and set you thinking. He will be very great, some day; don't you think he will?"

"I think he ought to be," answered Eninger, not knowing that the reply came in a changed and almost husky voice. For that afternoon at least, the pleasure of his *tête-à-tête* had been spoiled.

III.

Another fortnight passed, and London was nearly always wrapped in funereal hazes. But sometimes, when the fog was at its densest, wild yellow light would tinge it until all the air looked so elfin you might have said the end of the world was imminent. It had now become plain to Eninger that he would not sail for America that year. He might go to Paris or even further, but he would never put the sea between Alicia Delamere and himself until certain that Fabian's resolve not to marry her was irrevocably clinched.

She loved Fabian. He had made himself sure of that, and had suffered pangs in fully awakening from the effects of the Colonel's welcome falsehood. He had recognized the real grandeur of his friend's intended sacrifice. But perhaps because his entire nature was built on pediments feebler than Fabian's he had doubted if that sacrifice would ever be made.

One evening changed all this. Fabian entered his rooms, paler than usual and clearly agitated. He gave Eninger no greeting, but planted himself not far from the door which he had just closed, while he curtly said:

"I have lately been treated almost with open insult by Colonel Delamere."

Eninger, who was in full evening dress, and had been about to start in a cab for the comfortable little club, not far from Piccadilly where he often dined, looked placid and polite defiance as he answered:

"Really, one would suppose from your manner, that you had been treated with open insult by me."

Fabian tossed his head and smiled bitterly.

"If you call treachery insult, yes," he responded.

"Treachery?" repeated Eninger, squaring himself. "Come, now."

"The Colonel isn't always a trustworthy man," were Fabian's next words, "but in this case I think he has proved himself one."

"This case! What case?"

"You've made it plain to him that you wish to marry his daughter."

Eninger turned rather pale, and locked his hands behind him.

"Did the Colonel say that to you?" he asked.

"Yes. Do you deny that he told the truth?"

Fabian stood before his friend, inexorable as an accusing judge. Eninger scanned his tranquil face for an instant and then threw up both hands, half turning away.

"Good God, man," he muttered, "haven't you seen that I care for the girl? Because you reject her yourself must you keep everybody else from trying to get her?"

After so speaking, Eninger held his countenance averted. It seemed to him that an immensely long period elapsed before Fabian again spoke.

"I think only this," at length came the words he waited for. "If you did not see the crime of such a marriage as I saw it, you might have used decent candor in telling me so."

Eninger clinched his hands and replied, with quivering lips.

"Fabian," he exclaimed, "I accepted your prior claim. You renounced that claim —you told me so. But if this be not true, I retire again in your favor . . . Stop! you're about to question my moral sense in wishing to marry Alicia. That you have no right to do. If you will say to me now, at this moment, that you will take the girl, I promise you I'll withdraw from ever trying to become her husband. If you refuse to adopt that course, I shall hold free the field of my own endeavor. Can you, honestly, call this treachery? Before you accuse me again, weigh well your words. You've always prided yourself on justice. Prove now that you've not dealt in mere vaunts."

Fabian's brow was a cloud of storm as he stepped a little nearer to the speaker.

"Justice!" he exclaimed, with a passionate sorrow in his tones. "Can you dare to use the word? I've told you everything. You know what such a marriage may mean!"

Eninger slowly inclined his head.

"There are such things as childless marriages," he answered coldly.

Fabian stared at him in silence. If his look had been purely one of scorn, its object might have flung back hot resentment. But it was both more and less than this. It brimmed with an arraignment that seemed to search and scorch the inmost soul of the man who guiltily met it.

"As you will, Ray Eninger," he at last said. "We will speak no more of either treachery or justice. I shall leave England in two days' time; that I promise you. The field of endeavor, as you've termed it, is quite clear. There is my answer. What your own conscience and honor may say to you in the coming years I shall not presume to question."

He turned, after thus speaking, and opened the door near which he stood. As he passed from the room, Eninger was on the point of uttering some angry retort; but swiftly a great exultation replaced his ireful impulse. He sank into a chair, covering his face. The thought of what might now occur, dizzied him and made his blood bound.

Calmer moments brought him suffering. He perceived how he must have soiled himself in the sight of the friend whose respect he had treasured; for after all he was of too high-strung and delicate a fibre not to feel in full degree the shame of his own disloyalty. But a certain reparation might be made in the future. He began to build hopes on such a contingency, and to picture Fabian as a guest in his New York home. Why should this not sooner or later come about? Far stranger things had happened, and there were elements, qualities in Fabian which seemed all the more stimulant and tonic to him now that months of separation had again given place to companionship. As for Alicia's love, why should it not change its current, so that when she once more met the man who had set throbbing her maiden pulses he would seem to her only a vague image beside the dominant one of him whose name she now bore? And as for Alicia herself, surely to become his wife

must prove, should she ever accept such a
fate, more of blessing than curse. He would
guard her as the lid guards its eye. If insanity lurked like an ambushed bravo in her
brain he would keep the foe at bay with all
the spells his medical craft could conjure.
His vigilance should be sleepless and his
most potent spur toward the deepening and
broadening of scientific research should
spring from eager interest in herself. If the
world ever knew him for a famous physician
it would be chiefly through her precious
though unconscious aid.

He trembled, all this while, with dread of
Alicia's discountenance. That he should win
her, too, merely as the suitor with the well-
lined purse, was wholly repellent. She had
known Fabian first, and even his desertion
could not be expected instantly to turn
the tide of her sentiment. Eninger was
already schooling himself not to care very
much if the girl should become his with a
pronounced preference for Fabian; but he
hated to think that she might perhaps marry
him with no more human motive than one

of cold-blooded expediency. The old Colonel was of course his ally, and yet he feared
lest Alicia's father might either ruin the
cause by bungling, or else goad his child into
a rôle of self-immolating hypocrisy. After
some reflection Eninger concluded that there
was only one course to take—he would avoid
the Colonel altogether, and go straight to
Alicia with his passion and his promises.

He did so, a few days later, and the experience bred for him nothing but anguish.
Alicia answered him with tone and mien that
there could be no mistaking.

"I'm grateful to you," she said, in her fluttered and breaking voice. "I—I did not
think you believed—— Well, no matter,
though, Mr. Eninger. The—the fault may
have been altogether mine."

"The fault?" he queried.

"I mean that perhaps I—I led you to
think I cared for you in that way. And
if I did, it was very blamable in me—
very!"

"No," he returned; "I don't accuse you
of any coquetry; and the blame is all on my

4

side.   I should have remembered that Dimitry——''

"Ah, don't mention his name!'' she cried,
bursting into tears.

"You loved him, then?   You mean that I
could not replace him in your heart?"

"My heart!" she exclaimed, with a sudden plaintiveness that touched him past
words.   "My heart is broken!"   And so
speaking she slipped from the room in a
tumult of tears.

Eninger spent the rest of the day in dull
despair.   But that evening, just after he had
returned home from a dinner of which it
seemed mockery for him even to pretend to
partake, he was surprised by the appear-
ance of Colonel Delamere.

The Colonel, with his gauntness, and his
supercilious carriage of the head, and his
buckram demeanor, was at no time a pleasant vision; and yet a delicious little shaft of
encouragement seemed to pierce Eninger on
now beholding him.   Was it not possible
that the wine of hope might be borne him
even by so graceless a cup-bearer?

Hope the Colonel did bring, but not of a sort which his host greatly relished. "My good Eninger," the father of Alicia was soon saying, in his thin, chill voice, and with one bloodless hand stroking a spectral wisp of white whisker, "you have quite misunderstood my poor, dear girl, I assure you."

"You're mistaken, I think, Colonel. By the way, let me offer you a cigar."

"Thanks, thanks, very much," replied the Colonel, who doubtless had every desire to be gracious, though his nose continued in the air and his lips retained their pursed, imperious look. "Really, you Americans do manage to procure such superb brands. Now, my dear Eninger, I must maintain that you've read Alicia wrong—wholly wrong."

"You have been talking with her, I suppose, Colonel?"

"Yes; but not persuasively, not—a— coercingly; pray don't imagine it. She's irritated, stung, at the way in which Dimitry darted across the ocean. But, compared

to yourself, my dear man, she holds him as
a fellow of very trifling note."

"Then she's wrong," muttered Eninger,
and he meant the words from his inmost soul.

"Ah, don't run yourself down," admon-
ished the Colonel. "It's such a vile world,
my boy, that even so thoroughly good a
chap as yourself will have plenty of hard
things said of him by other lips than his
own! . . . But bless me, you've thrice
Dimitry's force and distinction. Depend
upon it, Alicia will confess as much to you,
also, if you'll only be patient and make
allowances for a girl's whims and freaks."

"I'd be patient enough, sir," said Eninger,
with sad austerity, "if I thought she would
tell me in the end that she felt a little genuine love for me."

"A little?" echoed the Colonel, with hilar-
ity about as successful as though it had
been attempted by a skull; "why, bless me,
Eninger, she's got a tremendous amount,
though it happens to be stored away somewhere behind her nonsensical shyness. Trust
me, now; I'm telling you plain truth."

But Eninger did not at all trust the Colonel. He had begun clearly to see of what foxiness this broken-down old idler had made him the object. The Colonel had lately met at his club a certain New York man who had known the Eningers, root and branch, for forty years, and could have told Ray's income to within a dime. Doubtless he had told it, and these recent profuse civilities were the result. The young physician squarely faced what he was convinced to be the truth. It was horrible to think of Alicia having steeled herself into an acceptance of his suit. It was almost as horrible as to lose her outright.

And yet had she not told him that her heart was broken? . . . He lay awake half that night, wondering what he should say to her if his feet strayed into Lincoln's Inn Square the next morning. Till ten minutes after breakfast-time he kept telling himself it was best not to go at all, but a quarter of an hour later he was quitting Bond Street for Oxford Street, and moving thence in an easterly course through the weirdest of amber fogs

The old square looked, as he reached it, like some misty and somnolent borderland between dream and reality. But when he had got inside the little Delamere house, and had found Alicia beside a fire in the small sitting-room and somehow appearing almost as if she had been expecting him, then every hint of illusion thoroughly vanished.

"I've come," he said, as he took her cold hand in his, "to ask after that broken heart." He smiled, though very sympathetically, as she withdrew her hand. "Do you know," he softly went on, "that I've been wondering whether I could not, if you gave it me, somehow find a way of joining the pieces together and making them look as though they had never been separated—never in the world?"

He did not mean a word that he said, and the spirit within him was very heavy as he thus spoke. He had indeed come to her hating his own weakness for having come at all. He expected soon to go away, and to go with an inward curse at his stupidity, to go with a vow that he would take the

cast-off leavings of no man on earth.
But Alicia smiled sweetly although sadly,
and he saw some kind of gleam in the smile
that made him drop into a chair at her side.
And then she told him, with a voice trembling less and less till at last it grew quite
firm, that perhaps she had been foolish and
willful yesterday, and that if he forgave her
it would put his generosity to test. He took
her hand, at this, and she let him keep it.
"Do you mean," he asked, off his guard and
covertly thrilling, "that you really *can* care
for me as—as I want you to care?"

Of course this was imbecility, but he did
not feel it then; and before any reaction had
had time to set in with him self-mockingly,
she had told him that she cared for him a great
deal, though doubtless not half so well as
he deserved. She made her confession with
an arch loveliness that blinded him to its
probable falsity. What could he do? He
adored her, and it was so easy to take her
in his arms and swear that she should never
know an unhappy moment as his wife, if
devotion could save her from one. After

that hour a seed of confidence was sown
within Eninger, quick to burst and grow. He
forgot to repine at the prepossession wrought
in his sweetheart by Dimitry; he remembered
only that there was a force of usurpature
in his own passion which sooner or later
would rule unchecked.

It is but fair to record at once that he did
not miscalculate. In a few weeks Alicia and
he were quietly married. They soon afterward sailed for New York, and the Colonel
accompanied them. Not that Eninger by
any means preferred this arrangement. The
Colonel appeared strongly to do so, however,
and declared that life without his dear child
would be desolation. This struck Alicia's
husband as probably most true, since the
poor girl had for six or seven years past
borne the worst brunt of their poverty, and
without her tact, thrift and pluck it might
have been a case of sink, not swim. The
Colonel gave no signs of grief at parting
from his native land, and after he had reached New York was housed much more comfortably in the pretty Forty-Second Street

dwelling rented by Eninger than he had
ever dreamed of being in the draughty old
tenement on Lincoln's Inn Square. But
forthwith he broke into cynicisms and in-
vectives that had America for their one
pitiless object. He seemed to see as wide a
difference between the customs of London
and New York as if he had been trans-
planted from the river Thames to the Yang-
tse-kiang. Everything here was vulgar,
crude, odious. Even the incessant glare of
sunlight hurt his eyes. He declared the
icing of sherry barbarism and the wearing
of overshoes idiocy. He said that it gave
him neuralgia to sit in one of our "tram-
cars," the people about him spoke through
their noses so aggravatingly. He affirmed
that our newspapers nauseated him, and the
filth of our streets likewise. He spoke of
"dear old England" and "this infernal
country" with a lack of restraint that made
Eninger recall how many of his kindred
had lost mental balance, and wonder if a
loose brain-screw might not account for his
sudden fanatical bias.

"You're so patient with father," said Alicia to him one day. "I thank you for it with all my heart!"

"Oh, I'm in hopes his nonsense will wear off," answered Eninger. "Besides, it's easy enough to bear almost anything from *your* father!"

He stooped and kissed her on the throat, and saw her blue eyes moisten as he did so. "Ah, Ray, you're too good to me!" she broke forth.

He took both her hands, holding them and staring down at her with a subtle hunger in his eyes. "No one could be that, darling. You deserve all that human kindness could devise for you. Unfortunately, in my case, that isn't much. But if the little I can do is only a help toward your happiness, I shall feel vastly encouraged."

"A help toward my happiness!" came her little flute-like cry. "Oh, Ray, what are you saying? Don't you *know* that I'm happy already?"

"Perfectly?" he asked, with his eyes still fixed on her face. He turned a little paler

as he put this question to her, though it is
doubtful if she saw him do so.

"Perfectly!" she answered, while a sort
of confessional flash leapt from her eyes, and
her lips remained parted as though she
were on the verge of saying more.

He drew back from her a little, still clasp-
ing both her hands. "Do women forget so
soon?" he said. "Do broken hearts mend
so quickly?"

She reddened, and her eyelids drooped. "It
isn't every woman who finds a consoler like
you!" she answered.

"And I *have* consoled you? Absolutely?"

"Absolutely!" she replied, and once more
her gaze met his. He knew then that she
had ceased to feel a shadow of regard for
Fabian Dimitry, even though he had not
been wholly certain of this until now. They
were alone together, and he caught her to
his breast with a stifled sob of joy.

"What a victory I have won," he said, as
he looked down into her smiling and blush-
ing face.

"You deserved it," she said.

The words went through him like a knife. He thought of Fabian Dimitry, who had loved this woman devoutly as himself, and yet had gone away from her with that calm sublimity of self-renunciation which braves being misunderstood, unjustly scorned.

"No," he said, in a slow and changed voice, while he took his arms from about Alicia's neck; "I did *not* deserve my victory."

IV.

He watched her health from week to week
—almost from day to day—with furtive but
eager interest. There were times when it
seemed to him that she had all the hardihood
of some strong rose-tree which may put
forth, if you please, faint-tinted blooms yet
rears them on sturdy stems. Again he would
be troubled by what struck him as an accent-
uation of her old restless manner. She
would sometimes vaguely assert of the
atmosphere on our side of the ocean that "it
made her feel *so* different," and once, after a
statement of this kind, Eninger said to her,
in a voice that quite hid solicitude:

"You think the air here doesn't agree with
you, Alicia. Come, now, confess."

He went to the arm-chair into which she
had thrown herself, and sat down, bendingly,
caressingly, at her elbow. It was dusk, and
they were waiting dinner for the Colonel,

who had condescended to walk out that afternoon in the detested New York thoroughfares, and who had not yet chosen to return.

"Oh, I shouldn't say *that!*" answered the young wife, shaking her head with some negative vehemence, "I've no doubt it agrees with me capitally. Only, it—well, it makes me feel so—so different."

"That is what you always end by saying." He took one of her hands in both his own, and then let one of his middle fingers glide along the artery at her wrist till it rested on a certain spot there. "How 'different' does it make you feel? Try and explain to me."

She gave a slight laugh. '"I don't know that I can, Ray, really! Well, I seem somehow to be *living faster* than I did in England. I don't take the same pleasure in rest; I rarely want it; and yet I'm sometimes rather tired, too—more tired, I think, than I used to be there."

"You're nervous," Eninger said. "This is a nervous climate," he added; "notoriously so."

"But I'm not ill," protested Alicia. "I'm

the exact reverse—except for that occasional
tired feeling. Often I've the sensation of
being *too* healthful!"

"Yes, I know," said Eninger, with his
face graver, perhaps, than he was aware of.

"Stop feeling my pulse as if I were an
invalid!" she cried, with a pretty mock-
petulance. She snatched her hand away
from his hold and threw it round his neck,
kissing him with tender abandonment. "I'm
so *far* from being an invalid, Ray! My new
life here has refreshed and fortified me so!
Only——" And she broke off, with another
laugh, clinging to him and peering into
his eyes, her blond brows embarrassedly
clouded.

"Only what?" he asked, mystified not a
little.

"You'll think it so absurd."

"Never mind if 1 do. I've thought you
absurd before. All women are, now and
then. Tell me."

"Do you know," she hesitatingly began,
"I—I have such a sense, at times, of extravagance."

" Extravagance?"

" Great! Of course you recollect how much
cheaper nearly everything is in London than
it is here."

"Oh, yes."

" Well, I suppose it's the change—the
freedom from that iron necessity of being
compelled to keep watch on every penny,
mixed with a sort of unconquerable surprise
at the higher prices on all sides of me."

"And this gives you the idea that you're
extravagant, Alicia?"

" Yes . . Oh, the feeling is so hard to
describe!" She closed her eyes for a moment,
and pantomimically waved both hands before
her face. "It's as though I *must* be wrong
—as though I *couldn't* be so well off in the
world as you've made me! You know what
a struggle those last three years in London
were, Ray! They begot in me the instinct of
saving all I could, and of longing to get
more—more! And now that I've all I want, the
old self-preservative impulse of the genteel
pauper still remains." Her face was lit with
smiles as she ended, but somehow a shadow

of apprehension crossed the mind of her hearer.

"I love her so dearly," he thought, "that I am not capable of being her physician. If she is ever ill—positively ill—I should distrust every drug that I prescribed for her."

But aloud he said: "My dear wife, your odd fancies do not surprise me. I might talk gravely about them and say that certain mental functions had been disturbed by those horrid latter years of your London life. But I won't, for——"

She lightly interrupted him, just then. "Don't!" she exclaimed, in her soft English voice that had such inalienable charm for him. She was facing the open doorway and his back was turned toward it. "Here is father," she went swiftly on, "and while *he* is near—Well, Ray, you understand."

Ray indeed understood that any incautious word against London life, whatever its form of depreciation or innuendo, would have taxed in drastic way the Colonel's gloomiest funds of sarcasm. On this par-

5

ticular evening, through the dinner that was
now promptly served, he showed himself in
a mood of especial bitterness.

"I hope you enjoyed your walk, father,"
said Alicia. "It was such a bright, crisp
afternoon."

"Bright—crisp," muttered the Colonel, as
he wiped a stain of soup from his moustache—far better soup than he had for a
long time touched in Lincoln's Inn Square.
"Say staring and piercing. That's about
what your Fifth Avenue was while I
tried to walk it. The pavements were full
of little clots of snow that was each one
a peril and snare. I suppose the only
thing that kept me from breaking my legs
was that beastly pair of rubbers with corru-
gated soles."

"Don't revile them, then, Colonel, if you
think they saved you," said Eninger. He had
drilled himself into one changeless tolerance
of the Colonel's morbid assaults.

"You must have seen a lot of pretty girls
with nice rosy cheeks, father," said Alicia,
"in such nipping weather as this." Her

words had the aim of dissipating irony, but they only fed it afresh.

"Pretty girls!" he grumbled. "Yes; I saw a bevy of 'em just now—four or five, all slipping along together like hoidens, and pushing each other with the maddest screams. I've no doubt they were the sorts of American girls who call themselves ladies. They were very handsomely dressed, in their silks and furs."

"Perhaps they were only very young girls," said Alicia.

"They were old enough to do indecent things, however."

"Indecent? Really?" observed Eninger. "Such as what, pray?"

"Wave their handkerchiefs to men across the street—men whom they evidently didn't know from Adam," growled the Colonel.

"Oh, they couldn't have been ladies, then!" exclaimed Alicia, with an uneasy look at her husband.

Eninger smiled, with a little impatient toss of the head. "They may have been well-reared girls enough."

"Well-reared!" cried the Colonel. "Oh, bless my soul! Come, now!"

"You forget," pursued Eninger, "that the American girl may do innocently what the English girl would only do immorally."

"I don't understand," bristled the Colonel; "I don't understand at all!"

"Of course you don't," said his son-in-law, coolly. "It would be rather surprising if you did. You know nothing of my country, though to hear you professionally abuse it one would suppose your slanders were based on some sort of real information."

Here Alicia cast him a beseeching look, and he paused, regretful that he had even said thus much. But from that hour the Colonel (who had reason to value his clemency) was more tactful in treating international points.

Perhaps there soon appeared causes of a social kind why the gruff old creature should regard Americans more blandly. Eninger had kindred and friends in town who at once joined forces, as it were, about Alicia and made for her a "circle." She swiftly be-

came popular, as all agreeable Englishwomen
do in New York. Her sweet face and even
sweeter voice were themes of loving rapture
among damsels whose younger sisters might
have been those very madcap culprits denounced by the Colonel. Eninger laughingly
said to her one day that he only wished he
had made as great a professional as matri-
monial success. Invitations of all sorts were
handed in at their modish little oaken doorway. Alicia was bewildered at meeting so
many people in so pell-mell a rush. "I
make mistakes in their names," came her
comic wail; "I blunder about them absurdly.
The women don't mind it, but the men are
so sensitive." She was all the more winsome—and especially to the men—because
of these bewilderments. Her complete freedom from affectation gave the dilemmas in
which she was plunged an enchanting
naturalness. She was so frank, and yet so
would-be courteous, that no one dreamed of
feeling affronted. And yet one afternoon,
at somebody's tea, when she addressed Mrs.
Wynkoop Westerveldt as Mrs. Tomlinson,

certain followers of the former lady thought
that she would never pardon so irreverent a
mistake. For between Mrs. Westerveldt
and Mrs. Tomlinson stretched a wide gulf—
one which no acquaintanceship had ever
bridged, and which was firmly guarded by
snobbery from undergoing any such process.
Mrs. Tomlinson was a clear-brained, warm-
hearted woman, who supported a large family by her pen, and yet found time to see a
little of society in a Paris bonnet and a pair
of *chic* gloves, paid for out of her own earn-
ings. Mrs. Westerveldt was a woman who
had in all her life scarcely even lifted a
finger for herself and never had done so for
anyone else. But one woman was merely
tolerated among the gay throngs that a
healthy, gregarious impulse made her now
and then seek. The other, rich, calm and
somewhat disdainful, was almost courted
like a queen.

Mrs. Westerveldt did not, however, show
Alicia the slightest pique. She was, indeed,
rather more polite after than before the
commission of Mrs. Eninger's error.

"You and I should know one another quite well," she said very sweetly. "I am an old friend of your husband's. Ask him about Gertrude Ten Eyck; he will tell you that we used to have many a dance together at the old Delmonico Assemblies in Fourteenth Street."

She smiled brightly as she said this, and it occurred to Alicia that she had a face of marble, with ice for its smile. She was undoubtedly beautiful, but did not her beauty repel rather than allure? So at least it seemed to her present observer, who had yet no idea of the immense condescension which she had now seen fit to bestow.

Later this fact became plain. The words of Mrs. Westerveldt had been delivered in a crowded drawing-room on Fifth Avenue, and near her stood several ladies and gentlemen who had the air of seeking her notice. But she did not bestow any upon them. She watched Alicia rather closely with a pair of languid gray eyes, and soon proceeded to say a number of civil things that were expressed with a neat, terse ease of phrase.

Not long afterward, a babbling little man of whose name poor Alicia was totally uncon- scious but whom she recalled having met on the previous day, told her that Mrs. Westerveldt was a great personage in New York and that people fought for the honor of darkening her doorways.

Eninger loathed kettledrums, and had begged off from going to this one. But when his wife mentioned to him that she had met Mrs. Westerveldt his face brightened nota- bly, and he at once said: "Gertrude Wes- terveldt? Dear, dear—of course we were great chums, once. She married a million- aire twice her age, who died a little while after the wedding."

"She looked as if she might do any cold- blooded thing like that," said Alicia.

"But she used to be very handsome."

"She still is," conceded his wife.

Eninger might have said more, but he pre- ferred to keep silent. In the whirl of mer- riment that now caught the town, he pres- ently came face to face with Mrs. Wester- veldt. They shook hands with one another

and talked trifles. Music was floating
through a great screen of glossy leaves just
behind them, and the large hall in which
they stood was dim by contrast with the
stately drawing-rooms beyond. Through
the doorway of one of these they could see
Alicia, stationed in a blaze of light, talking
blithely to a little crowd of men, with smiles
on her sunny English face. Two or three
male adherents were standing near Mrs.
Westerveldt, and one of them held her fan.
It was always like that with her. Wherever she moved there were gallants who
bowed their homage. Sometimes she gave
them freezing responses; just now she was
quite ignoring them. Her gray eyes, indif-
ferent and yet subtle, had lifted themselves
to Eninger's face and dwelt there intently.

"Your wife is charming," she presently
said, in her measured voice.

"Do you find her so? I'm very glad to
learn it."

"I didn't know you preferred that type."

"You mean—such a blond?"

"Yes."

He gave a slight shrug of the shoulders. "How can one ever be sure, in these matters, until the time comes?"

"You're right. One can't be. But you must take good care of her, now you've got her."

He started a little. "Oh," he said, "she can take care of herself."

"Don't be so very certain. Those English women are not like us."

He smiled as he watched her, so serene, with her chiseled, ivory face, her diamonds and her dignity.

"Not cold, like American women, you mean?" He felt so certain of Alicia that it merely diverted him to make this retort. Besides, he knew that it hid a challenge.

"Are we American women so cold?" she asked.

One of her retainers, at this point, dipped forward with the mechanic affability of his kind. "Your fan," he said, and extended it to her.

"Thanks," she returned, taking the fan and looking at him, but not seeming to see him.

"That is hardly *apropos*," she went on
to Eninger, paying no more attention to the
gentleman just addressed. "You've called
me cold, and here I'm supplied with this."
She unfurled it softly, and its wedge of rose-
tinted satin showed a little monogram of
diamonds at one corner. The gentleman
who had returned it did not depart. He
had evidently made his act a reason for remaining longer in her train and getting a
gracious word from her as the result of his
devotion. But she extended him no notice
whatever.

Eninger now leaned nearer to her and
said, in a voice and with a way that had
made him liked and courted before his marriage, when he had gone a great deal among
the fashionables of his native town:

"Perhaps the fan was returned to you
with a sarcastic intent."

"How?" she questioned, somewhat quickly,
for her.

"To wake the little real spark, concealed
—deep down."

"So very deep down?" she questioned,

with the pupils of her gray eyes momentarily wed to the pupils of his. "Do you then really think me—you!—a woman like that?" With the dulcet wails and tremolos of the music aiding her, she contrived to make her voice sound scarcely louder than a whisper to him.

"Ah," he said, stirred by old memories and swayed by the flare and prattle of the hour, "I think you (why should I not think you, please?) a woman without an emotion."

He saw her furtively bite her lip. He had said the one thing that the world had always said of her as Gertrude Ten Eyck and that it now averred still more stoutly since she had become Mrs. Wynkoop Westerveldt. It occurred to him, however, that perhaps he had done her a somewhat uncivil turn by his candor, even though it had borne a dainty sting of not unflattering flirtation. But, as if in sudden antithesis to the unemotional woman he had just called her, there appeared at his side a woman of strongly opposite type.

She was leaning on the arm of a gentleman

much taller than herself, and it would not
have been hard for her to find an escort of
this eclipsing stature. She was fair of tress
and tinting, and over-plump for her age,
which visibly verged on forty. She was
dressed with an undue youthfulness; they
had jocosely alleged of her for several years
that she flatly refused to be presented at
the Court of St. James because baby-waists
and sleeve-loops were impracticable in such
a surrounding. On her fat neck sparkled a
string of phenomenal rubies, and her fleshful
arms were banded with circlets of like gems
almost as precious. She gave Mrs. Westerveldt a short, intimate nod, seemingly taking for granted that it was returned, and
while drooping her small body toward Eninger, broke out in a shrill, amical, falsetto
voice:

"Your wife is just too *perfect!* We're all
crazy about her. She's a tearing success!"
Meanwhile the little lady had given his
hand a vigorous shake; and then, with the
effect of being dragged off by her companion—an effect for which he was no doubt

blameless, as her see-saw and almost tumbling walk soon evinced—she passed into a
living thicket of guests, grouped one or two
yards beyond.

Eninger turned toward Mrs. Westerveldt.
"There's your old aversion," he murmured.

"Don't call her old," came the reply,
while there seemed scarcely a motion from
the clean-cut lips that gave it. "She'd pardon anything except being called old."

He laughed. "It's so odd," he said. "In
the other days you detested her so, and here
I come back to New York and find you
meeting her as you used and detesting her
as you used, precisely the same."

"How can you say that?" said Mrs. Westerveldt, faintly smiling. "People only
detest when they feel. But you've just told
me that I'm a woman without an emotion."

He laughed again. "Oh, hate isn't an
emotion," he said; "it's a manifestation."

"Of what?" she answered chillingly, with
a reaching forth of her arm to one of her
attendants, who proffered his own with an
obsequious duck of the figure, as though

thrilled by such a favor. "Of bad breed-
ing, or merely dullness?"

Before he could reply she had moved
away, and while the possible sarcasm in her
placid words appealed to him, he asked himself if he had dealt her an offense. But her
displeasure or the reverse of it seemed a
minor affair now. In the time not long
ago, when she was a reigning maiden belle,
he had cared to keep in her good books.
But now all that was changed. Besides,
had they not often smiled together over her
antipathy for this rowdy little Mrs. Atterbury, who a moment before had swept past
them? It was the glacial Gertrude herself,
not he, who had given Adela Atterbury that
name of "rowdy." The two women had
always been to him amusing antipodes. Miss
Ten Eyck, with her patrician reserves and
her frosty *hauteurs*, had no doubt addressed
rather potently his own cult for the select,
the choice, the uncommon in all dealings
with life. Mrs. Atterbury had always
been to him a sort of unholy bacchanal
spectacle—a mænad in a baby-waist, and

without as much as one idealizing grape-
leaf. She was older by four or five years
than Gertrude Ten Eyck, and although
the new young social autocrat met her every-
where, she was even then married to her
present lord, Lewson Atterbury, or "Lewsy,"
as almost everybody called him.

"That woman is my horror," Miss Ten
Eyck had once said to Eninger. "The great
trouble is that I can't cut her. If only I
could, it would be quite different. But she
was Adela Ostrander, and for a Ten Eyck to
cut an Ostrander would be ridiculous. And
yet, as it is, she makes my flesh creep. She
has no more sense of her position than if
it were an old shawl. She drags it after her
through the highways and hedges. Why,
almost any reputable person who pleases can
actually know her. She's not the faintest
sense of what it means to keep oneself rare.
How can society deal with such people?
They're like traitors inside the gates of a
city when they've been born, as in Adela's
case, within gentility's limits. But the bit-
terest thing of all is that one must go to her

Wednesdays. Oh, the rabble at those Wednesdays! One meets there the most impossible persons. The dreadful little woman has what she calls literary tastes. I suppose she has. But as if democracy couldn't get along without thrusting itself into our good old families! Its field is certainly huge enough in other directions. All her set ever asked of her was to marry a gentleman and behave like a lady. That covers a good deal of ground. I grant; but birth has its exactions, and she's a living defiance of them all."

Those odious Wednesdays yet continued, however, and it was not long before Eninger and Alicia went to one of them. Mrs. Atterbury had had a fair fortune when she married, and her husband, though himself in Wall Street, had been the son of a rich silk-importer. Their added incomes enabled them to entertain finely in a home of smart presentments. Eninger had found that society had changed markedly since his brief relative absence. But he was unprepared to meet so many strange faces, even in the drawing-

rooms of Mrs. Atterbury. Among the faces
that were not strange he was keenly startled
to discover that of Fabian Dimitry.

Fabian looked paler and somewhat thinner
than when last seen in London. His brow
and eyes appeared to have gained, for this
reason, in the way of intellectual beauty and
power. Eninger and he did not once exchange
glances; this may or may not have been
chance, but afterward Alicia's husband felt
inclined to think that Fabian had observed
without seeming to observe him. How had
it been with his wife? He took occasion to
question her while they were being driven
home in the carriage.

"Oh, yes, I saw him," returned Alicia
composedly. "How handsome he looked,
did he not?"

A sudden little stab of jealousy pierced her
hearer. "You thought so, then?" he replied,
with almost harsh directness.

"Of course I did," she affirmed. "He *is*
handsome. Don't you agree with me, Ray?"

"Well—yes," he acquiesced. And the
carriage rattled clamorously onward, as

vehicles are apt to do over the stern-stoned thoroughfares of New York.

"It's odd," Alicia presently said, her suave English voice breaking in with melodious effect upon the strident rumble of the wheels, "it's odd, Ray, how much we can outlive in a little while!"

" And you've outlived——?" he began, not ending his sentence, but letting a sudden clasp of his hand upon her own end it instead. "Oh, Alicia, dearest," he soon went on, "you can truthfully tell me that there's no afterthought—no lingering sentiment—no——?"

"Hush, Ray," she shot in, with speed and yet very solemnly. " I was a girl, then; I'm a woman, now, and you've made me one. I think it's not a matter for us to talk of at much length. Only, love, I've this to say: Not merely can I look at Fabian Dimitry now without a tremor of the old feeling, but I caught myself watching him to-night (he never seemed to know if I was there at all, by the by) with actual wonderment that I should ever have cared for him as I did.

Yes, Ray, wonderment is the word—that,
simply."

As she paused he saw by the flash of a
lamp through the window that tears were
glistening in her eyes, and that the glance
which burned from them was passionately
wistful. In another moment he had leaned
down and seized her in his arms.

"My own—my treasure! You *are* all mine,
now! I've won you completely, at last!"

"You'd won me weeks, months ago," she
answered.

"And there's not a gleam left, not the
dimmest, of that old feeling for *him?*"

"No, no! not the dimmest. It's quite gone.
It's all been swallowed up in my deep,
absorbing love for you."

He had ceased from his fervid caress, but
he still held both her hands in the darkness.
One of them was gloveless, and that he lifted
to his lips, letting it rest there while he
touched it with short, soft kisses. And after
a little while he said, in a voice that surprised
her because it was so grave, with no trace of
joy in it whatever:

"I think he saw us both quite plainly to-night. Perhaps he waited for me to give him some sign—or for you."

"For me, Ray!" she exclaimed.

"You're still angry with him, then?"

"No—not angry; I can't be any longer .
And yet——"

"You don't forgive him."

"I—I haven't thought about it lately."

"You believed that he treated you in a really dreadful way."

"Ah, yes," she murmured, drooping her head in the dusk. "But why speak of it now?"

"Because," he said, "I'm certain that you wronged him."

"Wronged him?" she flashed out, old memories of pain and revolt seeming to waken in her. "How can you say such a thing? You can't be aware——"

"I'm aware that he loved you very dearly," was the interruption, "and that he gave you up."

He saw her form erect itself to the utmost where she sat beside him, and could fancy that he glimpsed an indignant sparkle in her eyes as well.

"Pray, for what reason," she slowly asked, "did he—give me up, as you call it?"

Eninger now inly cursed his own folly. Why had he thus let a conscience-twinge betray him into so indiscreet an admission regarding Fabian? If Alicia had never suspected the real truth, why should it be his office to enlighten her?

"Perhaps the renunciation was made on my account," he said.

"No," denied Alicia, with ringing tones. "Men don't do those things for one another." She caught her husband's arm with sudden and tense grasp. "I understand," sped her next words.

"Ray, it was because of—that taint in our blood."

He remained silent.

"Ray."

"Well?" he returned.

"It *was* because of that. Answer me! Am I not right?"

"Perhaps."

She sank back in the carriage. "I was
very stupid—I should have seen," he heard
her mutter. "There was never the least meanness about him—and he was the sort of man
who could have held his hand in the flames
and burned it off if some noble cause made
that needful."

These were by no means loud sentences,
but Eninger heard every word of them. He
folded his arms, there in the gloom, and sat
silently gnawing his lip. Who could say
what revulsion in Alicia this new knowledge
might produce? Suppose it undid the work
of months and left her once more in love with
him whom she had learned to despise as a
mere coarse trickster? A result no less
grotesque than calamitous—and yet what
wizard had ever yet been found keen enough
to predicate concerning a woman's heart?

V.

It was quite true that Fabian had seen
both Alicia and Eninger. In a crowded room
one can very often see without appearing to
look.

At first Fabian feared that he would be
obliged to quit the entertainment altogether,
for the image of Alicia set his heart leaping
and his ears humming in a way that made
him dread some sort of piteous public col-
lapse. But soon calmness brought its prized
relief. He then wondered, with a clearing
brain, what idiocy he might not have been
saying to the lady in whose company he had
stood. But among our drawing-rooms, as he
might have recollected, a brain may often go
wool-gathering without any decided chance
of having itself seriously missed.

His passion for Alicia was just as warm
and vital as it had ever been, and the wound
dealt him by his own act of self-sacrifice had

suffered cruel re-opening through this recent
meeting with her. He had not wanted to
appear at Mrs. Atterbury's reception, but
that lady had put forth quaint and voluble
entreaties which finally made him yield.

He had always disliked society, and had
shunned it in a way rare with one whose
name and place there are excellent as were
his own, and whose purse is the stanch if not
corpulent abettor of both. Society, he was
wont to say, undermined sincerity in the
sincerest people, and its effect upon his
friend, Mrs. Atterbury, was deplorable to
him in the extreme. Still, he would not
have Adela change her nature. She was full
of refreshment to him just as she existed.
He had never even remotely dreamed of being
in love with her, and the feeling that she
woke in him could safely have been called
good-fellowship. There was that in Adela
Atterbury which made him freely pardon
her vulgarity; but he would never have found
enough in Gertrude Westerveldt, on the other
hand, to have pardoned that lady her refine-
ments. The latter, whom he had met, was

merely an odious snob to him; but in Mrs. Atterbury, with all her loudness and eccentricity, he recognized the worth of a true-souled woman. It amazed him that she could endure some of the people on whom she smiled. Not a few of those who would have been called the most desirable struck him as the shabbiest in either mind or manners. "I don't understand you," she had said to him one day. "You're a democrat, you despise caste; and yet you mix with this quality a dislike of your fellow-beings."

"You're wrong," he had answered. "I'm not afraid of solitude, and I greatly prefer it to the company of people who jar upon me."

But she would always have it that he shunned his kind. There were moments when she seemed to him so prancing and skittish a figure that he could not help wishing she would shun hers instead of thus gracelessly courting it. The way she clad herself, and the intoxicated style in which she pursued pleasures that to one of her mind and age should have appeared wholly trivial, often pierced him with repugnance.

If he had felt a grain of sexual sentiment mingle with his regard for her he might have reproached or even hotly quarreled with her on this account. As it was, he not only tolerated, but tried quite to overlook her faults of manner and taste, while letting the rays of her exceptional intellect meet his admiring eyes.

Her life had often struck him as a tumult of anomalies, incongruities. Without apparent time for anything, she accomplished marvels. She patronized literary entertainments and amateur theatricals; she was ubiquitous at afternoon teas; she never missed a new play unless to miss it were discretion; she was never absent from her box at the opera on the Wagner evenings, and bowed before that mighty musician with no blind homage but a keenly clearsighted one; she read all the best books and a few that were good neither as art nor ethics; her charities were not only profuse but personal, and for her jaunty, buxom, ill-dressed little shape to pass from hospital to drawing-room was an occurrence of great

frequency. She possessed the qualities of a
brilliant, social leader, but it is doubtful if
she could ever have become, even in some
city less juvenile and provincial than New
York, any except the peculiar power she had
here made herself. A chief must not be too
approachable; she was extremely so. He
must not forget dignity; she remembered it
about as much as might a fire-fly. He must
not show himself too voluble; as someone
cruelly said of her, she had a tongue with a
biceps in it. And lastly, a chief must have
a little clan of retainers and adherents, not
averse to occasional bowings and hand-kiss-
ings; her associates were all on the most intimate terms with her, and thought no more
about the making of deferential salaams to
her than if she had been the wife of a city
alderman.

Since Fabian's return from England, her
warm sympathy with him as a writer of
plays had strengthened their previous friendship.

"You can do it if anybody can," she
assured him. "I guess there isn't a man in

this country who's got it *in* him as you have. Last night we had a box at Wallack's. A lovely company, but such a rubbishy play, my dear boy! The motive was tame and mean and stale; the characters were all weakly drawn, and not one of them developed through the dramatic and logical action of events. It wasn't art; it was cheap trick. It wasn't life; it was a tawdry lithograph of life, in a frame of such beauty and taste that you almost fancied you were looking at something poetic and fine. . . . Winnie Amsterdam kept gabbling to me all the time. He's such an ass, you know; but even he was better than the play."

Fabian, though well accustomed to her leaps from sense, and sometimes eloquence, into slangy trivialities, now coolly answered:

"It *is* so strange to me that a woman of your brains can put up with these fellows whom you yourself denounce as simpletons."

"Oh, Lord, we'd have a sweet time, we women," she exclaimed, "if we only allowed

clever men to talk to us. We can't afford
to take our pick. We've either got to poke
off at home or else we've got to cast our
nets for all kinds of fish. But, gracious
me! I don't want to complain. I have a
good enough time; I go in for a good time,
and I have it. By the bye, when I got home
from the theatre, last night, I pitched right
into that book of poems you'd lent me a
week ago. I was awfully ashamed of myself
that I hadn't had a speck of time to look at
it before. We were right here in this very
room, Lewsy and I. He wouldn't go up to
bed—he *can* be such a mule! It was after
twelve; we'd been blown off at Delmonico's
by Jimmy Vanderveer. Lewsy fell asleep
on that lounge, and snored horribly. I told
him this morning it wasn't only the champagne; he'd had a few cocktails in the afternoon, though he swore he hadn't. But then
you never can trust Lewsy about cocktails;
he *is* such a liar when he tipples. But he
can't fool *me;* I always spot him—*always.*"

"And the poems?" asked Fabian. "Did
you care for them?"

At once he was presented with a new Mrs.
Atterbury—or rather, not one new to himself,
for he had observed and been charmed by
her in this same vein many times before.

"Care for them! Why, the man has a
striking gift. He can turn a lyric like Heine.
He has the same sense of saying a thing as
if it must have been said that way, and not
as if he'd dragged his brains to find the
strongest way out of several others in which
it *might* have been said. There's so much
in that inevitableness of phrase and of intellectual process. You recognize it when you
meet it. You can't explain it, but the truth,
the justice, the nicety, the felicity, the sincerity, all strike you. This young poet
ought to live. I mean, of course, if he pre-
serves his ideal with the proper artistic conscience. What he still lacks, I should
say, is a secure instinct of selection. He
doesn't always grasp just the right *chute
de phrase*, and he doesn't always either
choose or grasp his subject as he might.
But there's a subtle native music in him
that delights. I felt it, in spite of Lewsy's

heavy snores, which were certainly not musical."

"Your criticism is truth itself," said Fabian. He looked at her and marveled at her queer, repelling, fascinating many-sidedness.

He had no friend who was so near to him in judgment and penetration of his own work. Eninger, he had often mused of late, might have told him things that even this curious and notable woman might not have hit upon. Still, Eninger and he were forever parted. He said as much to Mrs. Atterbury after the reception at which he had seen Alicia and her husband.

It was the day following that reception, and the hour was between five and six o'clock. His hostess had chosen to be at home to him alone, and considering her countless potential engagements, Fabian could not help holding this concession of privacy as one that teemed with compliment. It had never occurred to him—it never could occur to him in any ordinary course of experience—that she might possess the least tender occult

reason for such a gracious act. She was a
woman whose oddities had always been cele-
brated for pausing at the ranker kind of
scandals. It had been this about her deportment; it had been that about her attire; it
had been the other thing about her compan-
ionships and patronages. But about her
fixed fidelity to the man whose name she
bore there had never been heard even a
doubtful whisper.

Mrs. Atterbury's was a basement-house,
and the reception-room in which she and
Fabian were now seated looked from two
heavily-draped windows immediately forth
on the street. It would be hard to plan a
room of richer and yet more harmonious
tintings, or one whose embellishments (all
choice and costly) were disposed with a nicer
art. The contrast between this irreproach-
able room and the absurdly youthful and
tasteless garb of his friend, as she sat loung-
ingly near him with her small, plump body
half buried in cushions and her small,
plump feet placed cross-wise on a tufted stool,
struck Fabian as at once sad and comic.

7

"So you hated my Wednesday, you horrid thing," she had been saying to him, in affirmation rather than query. "Yes; you needn't deny it. Toward the last you looked not merely bored out of your boots, but agonized. What was the reason of it? Was it fatigue or disgust?"

"Neither," said Fabian; and then, with an impulse to confide in her, he told not only of his agitation at lately seeing Alicia, but of his former engagement and its gloomful end. His auditor gave him the most rapt attention till he had finished. Then she said, with a breaking voice and humid eyes:

"You gave her up on—on that account! And you *loved* her!"

"I loved her," said Fabian.

"It was saintly of you! There——" and she reached out one of her fat little hands. "Just give it a shake—that's right. I oughtn't to have called it saintly—heroic was the word. No wonder you know how to write good plays. You've got a nature so high that you can see from it right straight down into other people's."

"I did merely what I could not help doing," he returned.

"Oh, precisely. And so did Ray Eninger do merely what *he* couldn't help doing. But look at the difference. Well, you're crazy about her still, I suppose?"

"I'm still in love with her."

"Ever so much?"

He smiled. "Yes; ever so much."

There was silence, during which Mrs. Atterbury stared at a picture on the opposite wall. Suddenly she said, with a quick turn of the head toward where he sat:

"Come to Egypt with Lewsy and me this winter. If you'll say yes I'll start inside of a week."

"You woman of quicksilver!" he said. "Will you never tire of darting about?"

"That's no answer," she scoffed, not by any means playfully. "Come with us. Make up your mind, and come."

"Your husband in Egypt! He'd jump off the highest pyramid he could find, from sheer ennui."

"No he wouldn't. Lewsy's too fond of

himself and all his belongings ever to commit
suicide."

"I've settled down to work, you know, in
dead earnest. Travel and industry are sworn
foes."

"Nonsense," she retorted, biting her lip,
while her face clouded. "You'll just stay
here and eat your heart out."

"Not at all," he said. "I'll stay here
and try to get a manager and a theatre for
one of my plays."

She gave a nod or two of ironic assent.
"Oh, of *course!* And not make another
effort, I suppose, to see her even once again!"

"No." And the little word could not have
sounded firmer if his lips had been of bronze
and had spoken in some sort of metallic lan-
guage.

"That's hardly human," said his listener,
"though Heaven knows you've given proof
of being almost superhuman. You can't
but realize that she must still care for you—
provided she ever cared."

"Oh," he replied, "I dare say she despises me. Eninger, you know, may have

told her nothing as to my real motive in giving her up. And I—well, well, I some how could not tell her. I left her to suspect. Perhaps she did not, and if she did not, then, as I have said, she despises me."

He spoke these words with much quietude, but with that unconscious hint of inward funds of power that eludes all definition or portrayal. Adela Atterbury, as she watched him, thought how simply yet loftily great he had shown himself. "Ah," she now ex-claimed, "it's a shame that any woman should be so deceived. She ought to know the truth. It's not common justice to your-self that you should let her stay in ignorance of it. If she's half the true woman her face indicates, she'd not only pardon you, but——"

"Love me all the better, perhaps you mean!" And as Fabian thus made interrup-tion he spoke with a far more bitter accent than any which he often used. "Ah, no; she's a wife now, and pray Heaven she may be a happy one. I go out into the world so little that the chances are slender of my ever

meeting her again. Still, I shall always
like to know that fate has been good to her;
I shall like to watch from a distance the way
in which it shapes her future."

"I see!" exclaimed Mrs. Atterbury, pushing away her footstool and giving one of
her silken pillows a subversive toss. "You
will like to be a martyr for the rest of your
days. Ah, talk of virtue being its own
reward, and of the joys reaped from self-
abnegation! For a completely jolly life
commend me to the man who serves self,
not to him who slays it."

"I don't claim to be a slayer of self,
nor even its disciplinarian," said Fabian,
while the repose of his manner contrasted
oddly with the fret of hers. "But if both
were true I should expect greater happiness,
all told. For say what we will, that delicate, yet splendid moral hardihood which
renounces every pleasure tainted with evil
is more sensitive both to joy and pain
than the weakness from which temptation
seldom gets a rebuff. The vine that climbs
high has tendrils which the tap of one's

finger-nail could wound, yet which almost
might win vantage from a wall of polished
marble."

"Ah, save that sort of diamond-dust to
sprinkle over your plays," replied Mrs.
Atterbury, with a little skeptic laugh. "It's
brilliant, and even the gallery might like it
if used with due economy."

"Don't try to be cynical, my friend,"
said Fabian; "it's the one intellectual effort
to which you're clearly unequal."

Her face softened, and she looked at him
with a steadfast glow in her honest hazel eyes.

"I'd show you how kind I could be if *I*
were only that fate you just spoke of. Oh, but
the fates were three, were they not? Well,
I'd choose to be the one with the shears.
I'd use them to cut off Ray Eninger in the
flower of life, and make your Alicia a bewildering young widow."

"As far as I'm concerned, you'd be throw-
ing away your time," said Fabian, with a
smile that just hovered, and no more, at the
edges of his placid lips.

"What!" she burst forth, her sympathetic

gaze changing to one of suspicious poign-
ancy. "Do you really mean that you never
have moments of the least regret for acting
as you did?"

"I would do it over again if it were to
do," he answered. Then a light seemed to
break on his noble and gentle face as he
added: "Do you know what I often long to
hear concerning her?"

"What?" asked the lady, a little tartly,
and as if out of patience.

"That she's very happily married to her
husband and has quite fallen in love with
him."

Feeling thus, Fabian might have been
gratified by an interview which took place
between Eninger and his wife that very evening. Until then the husband had felt as if
a heavy seal of silence had been laid upon
his lips. For over twelve hours he scarcely
exchanged a word with Alicia. To glance
at her was to see how assertive were the
thoughts that engrossed her. Their dinner
was horrible to him.

They were alone, the Colonel being ill

upstairs with a cold. As soon as the servant had disappeared, Eninger resolved in desperation that some sort of stop should be
put to the terms on which he and his wife
at present stood. For himself, he had a
sense of grimmest foreboding. He felt as if
Alicia might at any moment say to him that
she could no longer love him in the least—
that her love had flown back like a humming-
bird to Fabian Dimitry. In such case what
should he do? She had become the air he
breathed, his sky overhead, his earth underfoot. If she failed him now, he would feel
as though he had but to stumble across
whatever blood-smeared threshold the finger
of suicide should point out.

When they were alone together he slowly
rose from his place at the small round table
and went toward her.

"Alicia," he began, hating the sound of
his own voice because it seemed to him so
timid, " I've an idea that you are very angry
with me."

"Angry?" she said, and started. " Why
pray?"

He sank into another chair at her side. "Oh, because I told you a certain thing and told it at so late an hour."

She appeared lingeringly to waken from a dream, and searched his face in a half-dazed way. Then she put out her hand and let it rest on Eninger's arm. The touch of her soft fingers, though merely the faintest of pressures, gave him a thrill like those known in the days of their betrothal.

"I have been very thoughtless, Ray," she murmured. "Not—not that I'd forgotten you—how could that be possible? But what you told me of *him*—ah! how greatly he must have suffered! I see his character in a new sublime light."

Eninger gnawed his lip. "And this has kept you so abstracted, so strangely absent-minded?" he asked. "You were thinking all the while of Fabian Dimitry. You were remembering that you had lost him, perhaps forever, and that I stood here in his place as his poor and unworthy substitute."

"*You!* no, Ray, no!" She sprang to her feet, and while he still remained seated she put both arms about his neck with an air of infinite fondness. "You have your own place, always, as my husband. I don't regret having lost him, as you phrase it. And it is not because of him that I have been plunged all day in meditation, melancholy, *what* you will. Ah, no, Ray, it's because of all that his act reminds me of!"

She palpably shivered, and her eyes dilated as if with sudden piercing terror. She clung to him, now, like a frightened child. "Oh, Ray!" she cried, "this curse, this doom! It has never seemed so possible, so near, so threatening, as now! If *he* felt that way, what danger there must have been, and still must be! The 'sins of the parents'—ah, how frightful a meaning lies hid in those words of Scripture!"

"Alicia!" cried Eninger. He rose and gathered her to his breast. "Oh, my worshiped! Who cares for those venomous words now? Only bigots and dreamers. There is no danger. You are always with me, and I watch you—I watch you. Your father hasn't been stricken. You've many chances

of release, of exemption. Kiss me on the lips,
my wife—again—again! It's perfect to feel
that you still love me!"

"Still—love you, Ray? I——"

"Never mind. I feel it, now; I shall never
doubt it after this—never, never!"

He meant the words, from his soul. While
he clasped her in his arms he had a sense of
relief that shot its bounds into ecstasy. But
abruptly, and before he could feel quite
assured of the truth, he discovered that she
was quivering with agitation. Soon her sobs
rang out, in the pathos of their incoherency.
She had buried her head stoopingly between
his arm and breast; but on a sudden he felt
her form relax, and then swiftly he knew
that she had swooned in his embrace.

VI.

She was ill for several days, though not in the least serious way. He insisted, as her physician, that she should lie in bed, and now and then he somewhat sternly opposed her desires to be up and moving about. The Colonel, incessantly watchful of her and but half recovered from his late assault of bronchitis, had harsh things to say of her illness.

"It's this beastly climate," he averred; "nothing else has done it, nothing else under heavens. They call it dry. Quite so. It dries up the human tissues. My throat's never before been what it is now. It's been bad, I admit, but it's never been—Oh, by Jove, there's a tang in the wind here that we poor invalids have got to grovel to! I suppose the natives don't feel it as we do. They don't —ah—*use* their throats quite so much. I mean, to talk through, you understand. They use their noses. Yes, their noses. I was

never so knocked up at 'ome as here—never,
bad as I've been time and again in the old
country."

Eninger scarcely heard the Colonel's audi-
ble musings. He was thinking at first of
Alicia, and then, just as he began to feel certain that her low pulse and dubious tempera-
ture had yielded to treatment, a sharp crash
of hurt beset him.

The failure of the great banking-house,
Auchester and Tyng, made him tremble with
regard to certain bonds and deposits. They
meant, for the most part, his pith and kernel
of income. He rushed "down town" in disarray, and found himself but one of a wild-
eyed throng besieging doors that had aired
for years above their lintels almost the solid
credit of the Bank of England itself. Nothing could be done; all to do was to wait, and
to wait was to do nothing, naturally, except
to palpitate. Alicia quickly caught the con-
tagion of his alarm, much to his regret.
Eninger had wild thoughts, as he watched
her anxious face, regarding immediate settlements upon her that would lift her from

depths of his own insolvency into secure if modest competence. They had already issued cards for a large tea, and a day before this event he found his wife tremulous, agitated.

"My dear Alicia," he said, "the entertainment is all right It doesn't trench deeply on our purse; it's a trifle, and pray only think of it as one."

"I can't, I can't," faltered Alicia. "It seems as if we were doing a most reckless thing, Ray. It seems as if we were flying in the very face of poverty."

He gave her certain details of his financial reservations and expectancies. They were not large, but he made them sound larger than they were, just for the purpose of comforting her. Still, they did not comfort, and when the day of the tea came she was unstrung, haggard, by no means herself.

Mrs. Westerveldt and Mrs. Atterbury met in Eninger's drawing-rooms, as they met in so many others. The festivity was really charming, with no trace of the gloom that had fallen over the fortunes of its givers.

"Your wife doesn't seem well," Mrs.

Auchester and Tyng gave him a new chance
for gibe and slur. "Bless me, I wouldn't
have thought it possible," he declared. "But
then there's a kind of American dishonesty
that's like your prairies or your blizzards.
It beats the world for size and strength."

The uncertainty of his position made it
harder for Eninger to bear. There still
remained a most irritant doubt as to just
how much had been left. Meanwhile Alicia's
health gave him other cause for anxiety.
There were moments when he told himself,
with a cold pang at the heart, that she was
falling under the same dread ban which had
been so often visited upon her race. Then he
would laugh at his own fears and call them
reckless borrowing of trouble. A wandering eye, a touch of pallor, an air of languor—were these of necessity the signs and
symptoms that waited on madness? Besides,
had not her father escaped, and why should
not she escape as well? Plainly, these losses
had been a shock to her. In her sleep he
had heard her murmur words that were like
a moaning protest against the potential

scourges of poverty. Then, too, he would notice her reluctance to spend the smallest amount of money for what was sometimes the most needed purchase. And yet he had long ago become certain that her nature was not in the least mercenary. This frugality, this pinching economy, distressed him, and he one day begged of her that she would strive to be her old self again. To his annoyance her answer was a burst of tears, followed by a sort of hysteric embrace.

"I—I want so very much to act more bravely and sensibly, Ray," she quivered. "But it's the hardest thing, I find, to get that one haunting thought out of my brain:—perhaps we may not have enough left to shield us against starvation."

"Starvation!" he echoed. "Oh, Alicia, calm all fears of that sort."

"I wish I could," she answered, with the big tears glistening on her cheeks and hanging from her lashes. "But oh, we were so near it once, father and I—so near it, so hatefully near it once!"

"Alicia!" cried Eninger, "there is no

danger like that now. Force the fear from your mind. We may find it best to go into the country and live, but surely that will be a long way from the beggary you've brooded over."

On the evening of the Westerveldt dinner she came down-stairs to meet her husband in a gown that became her charmingly. But after he had surveyed her costume for a minute or so, Eninger said:

"My dear, you have forgotten something."

"What?" she asked.

"Your diamonds."

"Oh, I thought I wouldn't wear them, Ray." The color mounted into her face and then died out again.

"Not wear them!" he said. "But they're really very fine. That brooch of my mother's——"

"Yes, I know, Ray; it's exquisite. They're all exquisite. But I must tell you that I—I've a horror of losing them."

"Losing them!"

"Yes. We—we need all we have now, Ray, and—well, I won't try and explain my queer feeling; it's better, no doubt, that I should not. But you'll understand, I'm sure, and—and humor me."

She was looking at him with restless eyes and a troubled smile, as he took one of her hands in each of his own. "No, Alicia," he returned, gently enough, but with an excessive latent firmness; "I will not humor you to-night, for I think it would be doing you an unkindly act. These nervous caprices are perilous things, my dear, unless we learn to master them. You must go upstairs again (forgive me if I speak in tones of command) and put on those diamonds."

"But, Ray," she began, "I ——"

"No, my dear; there must not be any refusal. Go." He kissed her on the forehead and released her hands.

She stared at him with an odd fixity for an instant, and then quietly quitted the room. Eninger flung himself into a chair after she had gone, with a long, heavy sigh.

What did it mean? Such a fancy as that! She, the daughter of a long line of gentlefolk, to be afraid of wearing a few diamonds because there was a chance of her losing them!

The young husband sat for some little time with bowed head and a sense of fatal despondency. He had had so much to torment him, of late—and yet what was the loss of every dollar he owned compared with any calamity to *her!* Just such queer freaks and whims as these meant in some cases the subtle approaches of mental malady; his knowledge of the human brain and nervous system assured him of this fact, and yet he could not be the physician he was and not realize that hundreds of people lived on for years with "fads" and hallucinations of a far more serious kind, dying at last in the full possession of so-termed sanity.

Alicia's entering step roused him, and he sprang up, to see her with that delicate, yet brilliant, change in her apparel which was precisely what he had felt that it lacked.

"You look a hundredfold better!" he cried. "That aigrette in your golden hair, my darling, is like the morning-star over Maud's garden,

'Beginning to melt in the light that she loves
On a bed of daffodil sky.'"

He laughed aloud at his own rhapsody, although the laugh had no really mirthful ring. Alicia was nearly speechless until they reached the Westerveldts'. There Eninger almost lost sight of her for at least three hours. He sat next to Mrs. Westerveldt while the palates of about twelve assembled guests were being tempted and tickled. This was done, as everybody agreed, with striking success. He had never seen his hostess more suave and yet more statue-like. She made him think of snow with a rose-colored light upon it. On her other hand sat the duke, a little dark man who looked like a Hebrew jockey. She was by no means over-civil to his grace, as Eninger could not help remarking. He forgot her coldness, her stony ambition, her pagan views of life, as he sipped the perfect wines of her feast and watched her fair, patrician profile.

Suppose he had married this woman, after all. Perhaps he might have done it; she had married Wynkoop Westerveldt

with a dash of wild desperation in the
deed which very few people were aware
of, but of which they said that he, Ray
Eninger, alone held the real secret. As
Gertrude Ten Eyck she had had a large
fortune. And in *her* veins ran no blood
tainted by madness. She might have borne
him healthful and beautiful children. As it
was, he must stay childless, with a wife who
struck a chill through him if she but passed
a restless night.

Thoughts like these were grossly selfish,
and Eninger loved his wife too dearly to in-
dulge them in any meaning mood. But he
had felt wearied and forlorn on coming
hither, and now there was a certain sort of
exhilarant balm in the words and ways of
Gertrude Westerveldt. Her own prosperity,
and a thought of his financial downfall, had
possibly combined to bring forth in him that
worldliness which so many of us hide at the
mystic bases of our being.

"If it were a matter of any moment to
you," he said, at length, "I should tell you
that your dinner is faultless."

" Does that mean you enjoy it?" she replied. " For your doing so must be a matter of moment."

" Ah, you're graciousness itself."

" And it's all learned by rote," she said,
between little mellow ripples of laughter.
"It's wholly mechanical, without a single
spontaneous touch."

"I don't understand."

"No! But you should. You know me so
well."

"Not half so well as I should like to."
He took quite a deep draught of some ice-
cold *brut* champagne as he spoke. Just over
the rim of his glass, as it were, he saw the
silvery gray of her eyes gazing at him, no
keener than would have been two mist-veiled
autumn stars.

" But you must know me very well," she
insisted, " or you would never have passed
judgment upon me in the grand way that
you did pass."

" I?" he murmured.

"Oh, yes. Burnish your memory a little.
It happened only the other day. You said

it in perfectly cold blood, too. Can't you remember it?"

"Oh, you mean——" he began, a trifle stammeringly.

"That I was a woman without an emotion." she broke in, her smooth and vibrant voice seeming somehow guiltless of any interruption at all. But instantly the voice changed, and she spoke with a new kind of softness—one with which rebuke was delicately mingled, like the first faint coolness of the dying season with summer's native mildness. "Of all persons you are the last who should tell me that."

"Perhaps I meant," he said, "that you'd outlived your emotions."

"And why?"

"Because you're such a great lady, now. Not that you didn't always promise to be—whenever you should marry."

"That is so queer to me," she answered; "for people to imagine, I mean, that one has ossified merely because one chooses a gregarious life."

"You call it gregarious?"

"Why not? I only go where I choose to go, but I see lots of people. I only wish they all pleased me."

"But it isn't easy to please you."

"I thought once that you found it easy."

He smiled the fleeting, familiar smile that long ago had secretly charmed her. "Oh, but I never was quite sure. you know!" he said.

"Quite sure?"

"Whether I pleased you or not."

She shook her head ever so slightly, and in her eyes he fancied he could see tiny rays that told him he was incorrigible, he was at his ancient tricks.

"Sometimes," she said, "I think you speak as if you wanted to ape the hollow *fadeurs* of men who are greatly your inferiors." She lowered her tones a little, though there was no need of this, for the wines were bidding the folk babble all about them, and harps and violins were making melodious a distant ambuscade of orange-trees. "Were you not quite sure if you pleased me or no," she continued, "on a certain August night at Sharon?"

"I recollect how you threw away a ring that I gave you," he replied. "It rolled off along the road, and although the stone sparkled in the bright moonlight, I never afterward found it. I think it must have fallen into that ditch. I wonder if it's there yet."

"If I thought so," she said, "I believe I'd go there and try to fish it out. I behaved so badly. But you might have seen——"

"Seen what?" he murmured, as she paused, and bent his head down so that a stray wisp of her hair touched his temple.

"My jealousy," she said. The two words were very low; he could just make them out and no more.

"Oh, of that girl?" he returned, and felt his heart beat oddly, perhaps from pure surprise at the audacity which this last little undertone had sheathed. "Upon my word, I forget who she was."

"But *I* haven't forgotten."

He sighed, and as he did so it seemed to him that the sigh was a wholly sincere one.

"I should have known this before," he murmured. "That you really cared, I mean."

"Yes?—Well, let us talk of something else."

But she immediately afterward turned to the duke, and during the next ten minutes or so Eninger found himself dealing in the merest thistledown of thought and speech with the lady on his other side.

"The duke thinks our climate so delightful," his hostess presently said to him, however. "Do you suppose that is only politeness?"

"Why shouldn't it be more? Our sunshine, you know, is a revelation to the English."

"But our icy blasts—what must they be? Alas! I know what they are to myself. If I stay here many more winters I shall die of neuralgia."

"So you've that trouble?"

"Frightfully, at times. Why won't you doctors invent something for us martyrs?"

"We're always doing so; we're always

trying it.   But each martyr requires a special course of treatment."

She looked him full in the eyes again, and on her lips lay a smile of exquisite sweetness which seemed flinging lovely challenge to all that the world had ever said about her being cold of heart.

"Very well, then," she answered, "won't you give me a special course of treatment?"

"I never mix business with pleasure," he laughed. "Still, to do you any service would be so great a pleasure that I'll waive professional etiquette for this once."

"And come to me on—let us say Wednesday morning at twelve?"

"Yes."

"Bringing with you lots of scientific knowledge?"

"All that I possess."

"It will seem so strange to have *you* feeling my pulse!"

"It may prove rather agitating to myself."

"Physicians must be above such follies."

"Unfortunately we can't help being men."

That evening, as they rode home together,

Eninger noticed a sharp change in the manner of his wife. Her reticence and gravity were gone, and a lively buoyancy filled their place. She had liked the dinner, but still more the guests gathered to partake of it. The Colonel met them as they arrived home, and to her father she was unwontedly garrulous.

"Never abuse American society again!" she playfully commanded.

"I never have abused it," said the Colonel, telling a falsehood for the sake of making an epigram "I've only said that it didn't exist."

"Ah," cried Alicia, "if you'd seen those charming drawing-rooms! And then the appointments in the dressing-rooms upstairs. They were——" She paused, and to her husband's ears the break-off in her voice was so abrupt a one that he looked at her with surprised inquiry. She hurried along at once, however, with new sentences on subjects new although similar. "The entertainment was altogether perfect, father; I'm sure you'd have said so. If there's any duchess in

England more *distinguée* than Mrs. Westerveldt, I should greatly like to see her."

"Oh, I've met dowdy duchesses in my
time," grumbled the Colonel. "They're
most of 'em only poor country-folk, you
know, that don't come up to London except
for two or three months a year. It isn't as
if they lived in their brown-stone fronts on
the Avenoo" (he purposely made his pro-
nunciation barbaric) " and were great guns
in the mighty but select multitude of the
Four Hundred."

A little later, after Alicia had gone to her
dressing-room, Eninger passed into it from
his own apartment. The door was slightly
ajar and in spite of his usual secure though
never obtrusive punctilio he had so recently
seen his wife that he now forgot to knock.
She was seated in front of her dressing-table
as he entered, and her eyes were fixed on
something in her lap. The instant that she
heard Eninger's footstep she looked up with
a startled air, and then he had a sense that
she was concealing something either within
her pocket or the folds of her dress. But

her act was one of extreme speed; all was over, so to speak, in a second.

He crossed the threshold with a sudden conviction that she had just fleetly hidden a letter. But whose? What secret could she possibly have from *him?* Then, like a flash, pride intervened.

" I will ask her nothing," he thought. " I am not even sure that it was a letter. Still, never mind; I will ask her nothing. A wife who deals in petty mysteries is always tiresome, but a husband who plays the petty spy upon them is tactless and dull."

Aloud he said, in the most careless of tones: " I merely came in to tell you that I shall sit with a book down in the office for a little while yet. It still is rather early— hardly more than eleven."

" Oh, very well," she answered, and he could not help marking, by the nearer view he had gained of her, that her color had sensibly lessened. He paused for a moment at another door from that by which he had entered, and glanced across his shoulder as if he were waiting for some fresh word from her

9

But she did not speak, nor did she appear
to know that he had thus paused. And
presently he passed from the room, going
down into his office among the medical folios
and phials of his profession.

VII.

The office was pretty and comfortable, with a fire of soft coal sparkling in the grate. Eninger now recalled that a few minutes ago the servant had told him of a gentleman who had called earlier in the evening but who had left no name, stating that he might perhaps pay a later visit. Eninger wondered a little who the anonymous person might be. Patients were not so frequent with him that he could hold their coming and going in light esteem. Heaven knew, he had begun to need and long for their aid.

It hurt him cruelly to think of leaving his present home for quarters more limited and less prosperous. The slight practice he had already gained would thus be unsettled and perhaps wholly destroyed. Borrowing he had always detested, and like most men to whom the arts and uses of business are unknown, he had only a slender acquaintanceship among those who are of the lending habit. Ready money was what he wanted and might go on wanting for a year to come; but seeking it from the ordinary club associate, who had seen him purely in his social relations toward life, was an ordeal from which he almost shudderingly recoiled.

On the other hand he was quite without friends of a more intimate sort. He had had but two since reaching manhood. One was Fabian Dimitry and one was a cousin, almost exactly of his own age, who had died and left him grief-stricken for the loss of a mutual love that time would eventually have paled and withered. Both his parents had survived only long enough to be dubious memories of childhood, and all the rest of his kindred were comparatively remote.

For a little while he allowed himself to dwell on the chances of some sort of assistance from Gertrude Westerveldt. Yet no, he at last concluded. But for a certain gleam of unexpected tenderness which had broken upon him from her cold personality like the polar light from a northern firmament, he might have found himself capable of making known to her his deplored straits. Now such an appeal, however, had become impossible. He could no more think of voicing it than of doing any wildly impracticable thing, such, for example, as applying to Fabian Dimitry himself.

He let this last thought float through his mind on a little breeze, as it were, of sarcastic humor. There was no one in all the world to whom he would not have been less desirous of applying than the man whose name had just occurred to him. It chanced that he sat before his desk, at this moment, with head ruminatively bowed, while one hand drummed a little unconscious tattoo on the lustrous mahogany. No doubt it suddenly struck him that to brood like this was futile, and he rose with the intent of bringing forth a volume from among his medical folios.

Directly opposite him, at the threshold of the near doorway, stood the figure of a man. Eninger at once gave a terrible start, for the total unexpectedness touched him with that wild dismay wrought in us by an accredited

ghost. But Fabian, advancing a few steps,
quickly proved that he was by no means
incorporeal.

"Your servant let me enter like this,"
came his quiet and well-remembered voice.
"I hope you will not blame her for not
announcing me; the fault was really all
mine."

Eninger made no answer. He was thinking that he must have grown very pale, and
that Fabian looked as tranquil as if he had
just dropped in for the most ordinary of
visits.

"May I shut the door?" presently came
the new-comer's next words. He lifted his
arm, half turning, and with a flavor of inter-
rogation in the gesture.

"Yes—if you wish," replied Eninger,
finding a voice. And then, after the door
had been shut and they two were alone
together, he added in as natural tones as he
could command:

"Pray be seated as well."

He saw Fabian sink easily into a seat and
was about to do so likewise. But he gave

another glance at that serene face, manly and
yet in a way feminine, with its lines of lip
and chin like the best that we see in sculpture
and with its fearless, thoughtful eyes aglow
beneath a brow of splendid breadth—another
glance at that once dear and still familiar
face, which had none of the romantic beauty
of a mere sentimental hero, but beamed with
spiritual and intellectual force as clearly as
an alabaster globe might beam with the
lamplight burning at its heart. Intuitively
it darted through Eninger's mind why this
man had come to him.

"Fabian!" he exclaimed, going several
steps closer to where the new-comer was
seated. Before he could do more than lift
his hand, Fabian had both lifted and extended
his.

Eninger seized it. Then, still holding it,
he slowly rose, and the two men looked full
into one another's eyes. What Eninger read,
or seemed to read, dizzied him, and soon he
had almost staggered backward. But in an
instant Fabian was again at his side.

"You're not well, Ray. I can understand

it. You ve had a hard shock. I came here to tell you that things need not be so difficult with you as they perhaps look. You see, I knew of your weighty investments with that firm—and then, of course, there is always gossip, in such cases, that one can't be deaf to even if he would."

By this time Eninger had got to be quite calm again, though he was still excessively pale.

"Fabian," he now said, and without a tremor, "you've come—I felt sure of it a minute ago!—with some sort of idea that you can do me service."

"Yes," was the answer. "I've come having that hope."

"Hope?" Eninger echoed, with what might be called the irony of pure consternation. "You, of all men living, were the last from whom I expected an act like this!"

Fabian gave a slow nod, as if he had foreseen some such response. "We should not lightly break old ties," he said. "For myself, I can not; they are not only too strong, but too sacred."

"And yet you had great reason to blame me," faltered Eninger.

"Well, I have reason now to pity you—and to help you (if I can), which is surely far better. I think that the something which it lies in my power to offer you, Ray, *will* prove helpful."

"Fabian! Fabian!" exclaimed the other; and he dropped into a chair, his head bowed and one hand slowly moving just above it, for an instant, with palm turned outward.

"It's this, Ray," went on Fabian. He seated himself at Eninger's side and spoke almost into the ear of the latter, whose head still preserved its bending posture. "You remember my old cousin, Mrs. Van Schaick, who lived down there in Second Avenue as plainly as a nun, and who had a million, everybody thought, which she would certainly leave to charity? Well, she died a week ago, and like so many other people, showed herself to have been reputed far richer than she was. Instead of a million, she left about a quarter of one, and only half of that to charities. To me fell twenty-thousand dollars; it seemed to fall from the skies. I've not the remotest need of it. You know how small my wants are. It's at your command—or less than that sum, if you prefer. Auchester and Tyng will pay up every dollar, they say, sooner or later. This you've no doubt heard, but of course the news can't repair your immediate losses. A loan like the one I'll gladly make you, *can*. Will you accept it? Mind you, there's no gift suggested; you'll merely become my debtor for a certain time."

Fabian paused. The man whom he addressed remained quite motionless, with his head still drooped. Then Fabian spoke again, and this time there had crept into his voice a new note, at once winsome and virile.

"I'd have written you, Ray, but I feared you might think that savored of . . . patronage—condescension, even. I thought it would be easier to speak than write. But I somehow find I was wrong. There's a sort of fog of self-righteousness about my coming here that I can't talk away. It—it gets into my voice and almost smothers my words."

"Oh, Fabian!" once more cried Ray, lifting his head. The light flashed on his tears;
they were few yet large, and at this moment
he was not ashamed of them. "That 'fog of
self-righteousness' is so like you! Nobody
but a being of your magnificent honesty
would ever have dreamed of using it against
himself!" And with the tears yet shining in
his eyes, Eninger gave vent to a great laugh
and flung both arms round the neck of his
guest. He had for years loved Fabian as a
friend. From that moment the man became
as a brother to him, and withal, as a brother
superior in every mental grace. His affection had always been blended with esteem;
it was now in a way delicately but clearly
haloed by reverence.

VIII.

That night was an almost sleepless one for Eninger. The stars had dropped golden into his lap and saved him from those detested changes fate was menacing. He could now live on in comfort at his little Forty-Second Street home, and use every honorable effort to win the wealth that comes with professional fame. Why should he not reap wheat at the end in place of tares? Other men with arms no sturdier than his own had not toiled vainly in the same huge humanitarian field. He would try; the odds were not against success. Meanwhile, this priceless Fabian had come to him, and the hateful debt which he had dreaded to contract in strangers' quarters would be a kind of glistening element in the cement of their repaired friendship.

And Alicia? In the morning, at the breakfast-table, when he felt sure that they were

quite alone together, he quietly told his wife
nearly everything. The Colonel always
breakfasted in his own room, and rarely
appeared until after twelve o'clock. But it
was the Colonel who gave Eninger a chance
of plunging into his subject, since Alicia's
father was usually in the habit, nowadays,
of dropping into the office between eleven and
twelve, if his son-in-law happened to be there,
and imbibing brandy and water under cir-
cumstances which he would no doubt have
considered social. They were not at all
times social to Ray, who wanted his medical
books and didn't specially want any brandy.
But *apropos* of the Colonel not having disturbed him on the previous evening (he
might have put it in the form of the Colonel
not having mildly shrieked American deprav-
ity to him in the stead of English impecca-
bility), the husband of Alicia found a cue to
this effect:

"No, your father didn't drop in last night,
but someone else did—someone else whom
you know—whom you know very well, my
darling."

"Someone else!" repeated Alicia, looking soft query with her sweet, ruminative eyes. "And whom I know? Pray tell me!"

"I will," said Eninger, rising. He took a chair at her side and spoke for a long time. He had forgotten the little occurrence of her quick, concealing movement on the previous night—or, at least, if he had not forgotten it, far weightier interests had driven it from his mind, and he was now rapt in the note and survey of these. He spoke amply, and also with detail and exactitude.

At last, when he had ended, Alicia rose, fluttered, visibly trembling. "He is to come here again!" she said. "And—to see me?"

"He has not asked it—he has indeed asked me that I should prevent such meeting," said Eninger, also rising. "But I have begged him to see you."

"To—see me, Ray?"

"Yes. Do you not wish the meeting?"

She clasped his hands in both her own, with her fair face brightening.

"Oh, why not? I—I should love to see

him again after what he has done for you!
Can't you feel this now, dear husband?"

"Now?" he questioned, with a covert smile,
"why *now?*"

She tossed her head as if a flower were
tossing in the sun, and he watched the tender
assieging color as it filmed yet did not dye
her virginal face.

"Oh," she exclaimed, "after all I've told
you! You remember? The sentiment I had
for him—it's gone—quite gone."

He put his arms about her and kissed her,
while he said: "Am I not certain of it,
dearest? You shall see him soon. No matter
about *his* sentiment. I dare say it may not
be gone. But I trust him so utterly. How
can I help trusting a man like that?"

Within the next fortnight an event occurred
in Eninger's household which he would have
been amazed to learn of if any fairy had
prophesied it. Fabian Dimitry went to live at
the home of his old friend.

"Good heavens, man, how *did* it happen?"

asked Mrs. Atterbury of Fabian, in a frenzy
of amazement.

"I scarcely know, myself," he answered.
"It seems now as if I must have dreamed it."

"*Her* idea, no doubt," said the little lady
dryly.

"She was very good to think of it. I
refused again and again, but——"

"She persuaded you over, at last. I see.
But my dear fellow, the whole thing is preposterous. If you put it in one of your
plays people would laugh at you. And pray,
are you getting along comfortably in Forty-
Second Street?"

He smiled at the quaint sarcasm in her
voice and look. "Very," he returned.
"And why not? With her the old romance
is completely dead and the new romance has
begun."

"Hm—are you quite sure of that?"

"I am absolutely certain."

"That sounds convincing. And about
yourself. In what stage of development or
decay is *your* romance?"

Fabian closed his eyes for an instant, like

one who muses. "I try to forget that I was
ever engaged to Alicia Eninger."

"Ah," laughed Mrs. Atterbury, softly but
a little cruelly, "you try to forget? And do
you succeed?"

"I hope so. It often seems to me that I
do. They are very happy together, and I
watch their happiness. I have not a near
relation in the world; for years Ray Eninger
was closer to me than any kinsman left alive.
It is a great pleasure to see his face and hear
his voice again. We have long and enjoya-
ble talks. Alicia will sometimes merely
listen, and sometimes she will break into the
converse in either a playful or serious vein.
I think the old Colonel is our one discordant
spirit."

"A horrid old creature," said Mrs. Atterbury; "he looks like a death's-head, and has
glassy eyes, and a voice like the ghost's in
Hamlet. I've caught a glimpse of him.
But he's evidently a man of the world. He
sees how monstrous is the present situation.
Or am I wrong in so stating?"

"'Monstrous' has indeed a violent sound,"

10

said Fabian, with that steady eye and calm
voice by which great and pure natures are
enabled to visit rebuke upon triflers too
rashly seeking it.   "I don't know if you are
wrong, however, as to the Colonel's motive
for ill-humor.   But then this country has
made him acrid from the first.   Nothing
could happen here that would wholly please
him."

It was on the verge of Mrs. Atterbury's
lips to exclaim, "Hardly anything could
happen here that *ought* more to *dis*please
him;" but Fabian, by the very dignity of his
gentleness, often blunted even her audacities.
And besides, as she would sometimes almost
passionately tell herself, she was very dearly
fond of him, and next to "Lewsy" there
was no man for whom she had ever got so to
care.   Considering that there were a great
many men and women in the world for whom
her large, warm, hospitable nature cared
extremely, this attitude flavored of rather
pungent compliment.

She was not always confidential with her
husband.   Now and then it was doubted

among her friends as to whether she placed
"Lewsy" quite so high in her affections as
she professed. The gentleman was a woe
and an alarm to some people; to many
others he was a fellow of great companiona-
bility and charm. Mrs. Atterbury chose
now to tell him of Fabian's recent action,
with a few graphic words that put the whole
case in lucid colors. Lewson Atterbury
threw himself back in his chair and roared
with mirth when the full idea had become
clear to him. He was as plump as his wife,
with a blond mustache too large for his head,
and with a head too small for his corpulent
and rather comic body.

"That's you—that's just *you*, to dare go
for him, Ad, because he'd got himself into
such a mess. Nobody but you would have
had the cheek to tackle a man when he'd
behaved like such a simpleton."

Mrs. Atterbury tossed her head impa-
tiently. "I didn't tackle him, Lewsy, as
you term it, and I didn't say anything about
his being a simpleton."

Her husband thrust both hands into his

pockets and lowered his head, slowly shaking it sideways. He never replied to his wife when she openly snubbed him. He had always thought Fabian Dimitry a "crank;" he thought everybody a "crank" who was not entirely commonplace, like himself. And yet, in certain ways, he was not at all commonplace. He stood forth strikingly in one respect, at least: all his geese were swans, and all his personal surroundings perfection.

"Cook!" he would say, if the question of home cookery was proposed. "I don't believe there's a woman in New York that can beat ours." And then he would narrate wondrous exploits on the part of this culinary Catharine the Great. With his butler, his office-clerks, even his porters, it was the same. Until discharged they were all nonpareils of worth and wit. Somebody had said, not long ago, that there was mercy for his friends in the fact of his being childless, as the virtue and intellect of any child born from him would have been trumpeted with agonizing zeal. But as it was, Mrs. Atter-

bury filled the place of that unbegotten off-
spring. There were men who had their reasons not to treat Lewsy uncivilly, yet who
turned chilly and felt an inward trembling
when he began with "My wife." His fund of
anecdotes concerning her was fathomless.
From her powers of repartee to her benign
charities, he had stories to tell of all the
shining attributes that made her unique.

"It is so charming to hear him sound
her praises," this or that wife would
say, always taking care to say it with a
touch of plaintiveness if her husband chanced
to be within ear-shot.

But Mrs. Westerveldt, who hated her
cousin Atterbury as we know, and who
thought Lewsy but a degree or so above one
of her footmen, smiled skepticism at these
eulogies. "He merely says nice things of
his wife," she asserted, "because Adela is
married to *him*. That's the only reason. If
Adela died and he were to marry another
woman, then *she* would begin beaming with
excellences, just the same."

Fabian had been quite right in calling

Colonel Delamere the discordant spirit of
Eninger's new household. The Colonel
might have shaken hands with Mrs. Atterbury and her Lewsy on the entire abomina-
tion of Fabian being permitted to enter his
son-in-law's home. He was ignorant of the
help which Eninger's old friend had brought,
or perhaps his disgust might not have been
so acute. But as it was, " Why, bless my
soul," he said to Alicia, "are there any such
things in this horrid country as propriety and
deportment? Is the marriage tie respected at
all? I've heard that divorces grow on trees
here. Do you suppose, you foolish girl,
that you're not sticking your head right into
the lion's jaws? Besides, what did this fellow do? Didn't he jilt you like a scamp?
Good God—are these American morals? It
will never do; nothing but deviltry can come
of it . . . American deviltry," finished the
Colonel, "which has got a particular flavor
and odor of its own."

To which highly sane and sage remarks
Alicia answered by putting her hand on her
father's arm and saying to him, with a good

deal more decision than most English daugh-
ters employ toward their parents, or than
she herself had been wont to employ toward
hers in former times:

" Father, you hurt and grieve me by words
like these. I love my husband very loyally
and dearly; I don't think there can be much
danger of the sort you mean to a woman
who feels like that. Then, as for Fabian
Dimitry, I've nothing to forgive. He never
jilted me; there's a complete understanding
between us——"

" Oh, there is!" shot in the Colonel, with
a vicious flash in the roll of his worldly old
eyeballs.

" Yes, father, and we want to be very
happy here. I hope you will aid and not try
to thwart us in our wish. There—there are
times when *I* am not happy," pursued Alicia,
with altered voice and a sudden trembling
of the lips. " I can't just explain. I suppose it's a nervous illness of some kind. I
often feel as if—but no matter. Only, I
beg you will not stand in the way of our
having a tranquil home. Peace, quiet,

nothing to jar and fret one! Oh, that is so
sweet! And perhaps it will make me better
—give me a release from certain foolish fancies and broodings that I want *so* much to be
rid of!"

Her last words were almost a sob. The
Colonel stared at her for a moment, and as
he perceived how swiftly her manner had
changed from composure to disarray, it is
possible that unwelcome reminders and
impressions may secretly have startled him.

"It's this infernal climate that's making
you nervous," he presently grumbled. "You
were never a bit so at home. Everybody is
bristling with nerves over here, though. I
wish Ray would take the wreck of what
those banker-thieves have left him and sail
back to the dear old country. We could
live in good style then on half what it costs
us to live now." And as the Colonel spoke
that last sentence he leaned airily backward,
lifting his eyeglasses and giving his bony
shoulders a faint, patrician shrug. You
would have said that he had just been
referring to moneys of his own which a

foolish son-in-law had chosen quite rashly
to expend.

Notwithstanding his hostile pose, however, the domestic peace which Alicia had
mentioned as so desirable appeared now to
reign undisturbed. Just before coming to
dwell under Eninger's roof, Fabian had discerned a glimmering chance as regarded the
production of a play at a prominent New
York theatre. During several evenings, when
no engagement claimed Alicia and her husband, he read them this play, and read it
with striking force and point. They were
both fascinated by its fine literary style and
its rare dramatic value. It had not a line
that verged either upon melodrama or farce.
It was piercingly true to nature, and though
at times full of that gloom which clothes
pregnant human problems, intervals of glow-
ing comedy here and there brightened it, like
patches of sun on a shadowed lawn.

"The play," said Eninger, after fully
hearing it, "is a work of excessive power. I
know of nothing modern and in English that
may compare with it. But would it lure our

usual theatre-goers! Indeed, might not its firm and harmonious art possibly repel them?"

"Ah, no, no!" exclaimed Alicia, whom the work had fascinated. "A play like that would create its own audiences."

"You may be right," said her husband. He turned to Fabian. "And there is really a hope that the Academic Theatre will bring it out?"

"The manager wishes to talk with me to-morrow," replied Fabian. "I am assured by an agent of his that he greatly admires my drama. But it is by no means formally accepted."

The Academic had been for some years past a highly successful theatre. It seldom produced native plays, however, which is but another way for stating that it was a New York theatre of prominence. What it did produce was staged with great skill and taste, besides being performed by a company of talented and supple artists. The manager, Mr. Lascelles, was a man of noted sagacity in business, with a little nimble frame and eyes like small black brilliants. But it had been said of him that he knew really nothing about the artistic or practical value of a play, and that without his counsellor, Mr. Belsize, he would never have raised the Academie to its present renown.

Mr. Belsize must have heard these tales, but he chose discreetly to ignore them. He was a man much larger of build than his employer, and one who could not appear uncovered without an aspect of almost spectacular picturesqueness. His eyes were dark and radiant, but were made more so by a curly crop of snow-white hair. Prematurely blanched, these locks crowned his somewhat ruddy complexion with an effect that brought to mind pictures of old French courtiers. But such illusion, if perpetually being created, was perpetually being destroyed as well: for an immense ink-black moustache curved along either of his cheeks and wrought sensational contrast with the hair above it. Mr. Belsize's nationality had somehow never transpired. When asked it, he was inclined to give evasive responses,

and his repute for all sorts of diplomatic
speech had long been securely founded. He
spoke French glibly, but not well enough to
have been born a Frenchman, and his English had a frequent cockney ring; but over
every tone and phrase that he used there
hovered (at least to Fabian's thinking) the
light spell of an etherealized "brogue." If
it were true that he was *au fond* an Irish-
man, then not a little of his adroit and facile
cleverness could be thus explained. Certain
critics affirmed that he had mutilated Dumas
and massacred even poor flamboyant Sardou
in his adaptations of these authors for the
Academic. But on the other hand he was
not without adherents who praised his quick.
perception of just what the New York public
needed and his complete efficiency in the
service of Mr. Lascelles.

It was the latter gentleman who first
received Fabian at the theatre on the morning of his visit there. The desk at which
Mr. Lascelles sat was rather plenteously
littered with play-bills and rolls of paper
which might have been rejected plays; but

for the most part there was hardly any real difference between this private managerial office and a like sanctum of merchant or broker. The wiry little man with the acute eyes offered a chair to Fabian, took a chair himself, and then looked studiously at one of his own boot-toes while he said:

"I liked your play very much, Mr. Dimitry. You must excuse my keeping it so long, but that can't be avoided at the Academic. We receive so many plays—so many hundreds, I might say thousands—every year."

"Really as many as that?" said Fabian, in his frank, serious way. "You must then employ quite a corps of readers."

This would not have been called by the foes of Mr. Lascelles at all a happy remark. He had too often been accused of keeping native, unperformed plays a twelvemonth and then returning them with the admission that pressure of business had made their perusal "as yet" impossible.

"A large corps of readers?" he replied, with a flurry in his mien that he quickly con-

trolled. "Oh, that's not necessary. You see,
so many of them are hopelessly bad. Most
of them need but to be glanced at on account
of this extreme badness."

Fabian nodded, but inwardly doubted. He
could not bring himself to believe that out of
multitudinous manuscripts yearly received
from a body of people as intelligent in countless respects as were his fellow-countrymen,
most of the offerings had so slight merit that
merely a critical glance could decide their
claims. He said nothing, however, and Mr.
Lascelles quite soon continued, with a caressing slide of one slender hand over one slim
knee :

"Besides, you know, Mr. Belsize is the
judge in whom I place most trust. Your
play happened to drift under his observation.
He likes it." Here for the first time Mr.
Lascelles looked Fabian straight in the eyes.
"He likes it very much indeed."

"I'm glad to hear that," said Fabian, with
heartiness but not a trace of exultation.
Indeed, he was to this manager, as he would
have been to most others in the same town,

a novel sort of dramatist. He was not in any process of half-genteel starvation, and a serene loyalty to art, rather than any feverish worriment about future bread, formed the motive of his present dealings.

Doubtless Mr. Lascelles had already grasped and weighed this fact. "Mr. Belsize thinks, however," he proceeded, "that your play, fine as it is, requires certain alterations before it can be accepted by the Academic."

Fabian appeared to meditate for a moment. He had been a very close student all his life of the best dramatic standards in the best of modern dramatic schools. Many of the great French masterpieces of this century he had seen played in Paris again and again. Every line of the work under discussion he had brooded óver with the love a sculptor feels for the marble he reverently chisels. Each character he had thought out with care and colored with a logic and probability borrowed from nature itself. The word "alterations" jarred upon him with a cruel crudity. He had never known a throb of vanity in his life, but he now questioned of himself: " What can be altered in any part of my play without hurting the whole? Is it possible that after my months of steadfast heed some new eye may sweep itself over the task and find flaws there which I failed to note?"

Aloud he said to Mr. Lascelles: " I don't think I quite understand you. Will you kindly explain these proposed alterations?"

" I dare say Mr. Belsize can do so better than I," returned Mr. Lascelles, as if there were some doubt on this latter subject. There was indeed no doubt whatever, since the manager had but power to look at a play through one purely commercial lens. For him what was good or great was what the public paid down its money at the Academic box office liberally to see. And in touching an electric bell and summoning his able familiar, Mr. Belsize, he gave signs of at least a temporary retirement in that gentleman's favor.

Mr. Belsize soon appeared and shook hands with Fabian, whom he had met rather briefly a few days before. Mr. Lascelles now quitted his chair with an agile little spring, and told Fabian that he would leave him with the new-comer. "I'm sure," he added, "that you and he will reach a prompt understanding." And then Mr. Lascelles vanished through a side door, no doubt being very far from yet even dreaming that an American playwright would not leap at the chance of having his work produced in almost any shape whatever, provided it actually got itself before the footlights.

Mr. Belsize had a more romantic and theatric look than when Fabian had last seen him, for the contrast between his colorless hair and raven moustache was accentuated by a fly-away bow of scarlet silk at his throat. "I am charmed with your play!" he exclaimed, and passed one hand through his white curls. "It shouldn't be touched; it should go on precisely as you have written it. You've composed a masterpiece, a classic. Surely, my dear sir, you're a student—I don't say an imitator, but a student, mind —of Émile Augier in France."

11

"I've tried to study all that is best in the French dramatic writing of the time," replied Fabian. "I suppose Augier is not to be escaped when one does that."

Mr. Belsize threw up both hands as if in lamentation. "Escaped! Ah, you should see how they escape him here. I don't believe you've an idea of how he shoots over people's heads. Dumas is very much the same. Sardou, no. But why? Because he's very often full of clap-trap; he uses red-fire where a true artist would use sunlight, starlight, moonlight. Now I want you to let me put a little red-fire into your play. I see precisely the places where it can be introduced." And then Mr. Belsize went into details.

Fabian listened with an occasional mild shiver. The speaker was very glib, and at times almost eloquent. He soon revealed that this "red-fire," which he had talked of with such careless contempt, was dearer to him (art or no art) than the light of sun, moon or star. In his proposals that this or that scene should be ruthlessly vulgarized,

he betrayed, by the very earnestness with
which his suggested changes were expressed,
a warm if secret sympathy with the changes
themselves. Fabian, with his native *flair*
for honesty, soon perceived this. He soon
felt that the whole man somehow rang
wrong. Perhaps he had once really had an
artistic sense, which the sad state of the
modern theatre and the incessant require-
ments of popular attractions had now par-
tially smothered. But no man, his listener
felt convinced, could coldly announce himself capable of such assassinating and devas-
tating work as this, unless his ideal had
either been sham from the first or had been
tumbled into the mud by an acquired van-
dalism.

"There," at last affirmed Mr. Belsize,
"that about hits off, in general outline,
what the Academic would like to make of
your play. After all, the *idée mère* of the
thing would remain thoroughly yours.
What we want to do is to ice the plum-cake
—to draw the big crowds. We've got to do
that. Merely dramatic effects don't take

the dollars out of their pockets. The fine
scenes in the '*Fils de Giboyer*' or the
'*Gendre de Monsieur Poirier*' go for nothing here . . . Now see," and Mr. Belsize
leaned forward, with his voice growing con-
fidentially guttural; "I've got a perfect idea
of just what can be done with your play.
I'll make it a go—a big go. *You* couldn't,
for you're not up in the show-business.
And here it's either the show-business or it's
flat failure. People in this country hate literature on the stage as they hate a cat walking across it. They laugh at the cat, it's
true; but they laugh at literature as well,
only with less charity. They're tired with
the tremendous push and hurry of their
daily life. They want to be waked up—to
be nipped." And with a large, white, well-
tended, muscular hand he gently seized a
segment of Fabian's trousers between thumb
and forefinger, just at the region of the
knee.

Fabian broke into a laugh. "I certainly
should not care to do the nipping you
speak of, Mr. Belsize," he said. And then

a certain artist-born thought—a thought con-
nected with the desire to observe human
nature wherever and whenever found—made
him add, in his usual graceful, reflective way:
"But if you should undertake in my manuscript the collaborative rôle you have indi-
cated, would not you wish (I do not refer at
all to my own feelings, pray observe) that
your name should appear as joint author
with myself?"

Mr. Belsize sank backward and raised both
hands, agitating them with an air of extreme
deprecation. "Oh, my dear Mr. Dimitry,"
he exclaimed, "I wouldn't for the world have
you dream of so foolish a thing. I!" and he
tapped his broad chest until the volatile-
looking scarlet neck-tie vibrated. "I am
simply a mere play-patcher—nothing else.
I know what bells and gew-gaws are liked
by that big baby called the public. A *col-
laborateur* with you—absurd! My offices
would in no sense make me worthy of it."
Here he gave a sudden start, and touched his
forehead as though a new idea had just
broken upon him. "But in a pecuniary

sense—ah, that is different. I should ask
(and I am sure you would be generous
enough to give) a—er—consideration out
of the royalties paid over to you by Mr. Lascelles . . . let us say one thousand dollars.
From your royalties you would each day de-
duct ten dollars, let us also say, until the
sum just named was reached." At this
point he shrugged his shoulders and rolled
his eyes toward the ceiling. The effect was
operatic, and he looked for an instant as if
he might be some Italian tenor in the melodious throes of "*Spirito gentile.*" "I would
willingly do my share of the work," he continued, "for no return whatever. But one
must dine. Mr. Lascelles gives me my
salary, of course, but you know the enor-
mous expenses of New York life."

"They are certainly great," said Fabian,
who was amused. He had yet to learn how
the stage in this country is infested with
cormorants like Belsize; how almost every
successful foreign play produced here is bat-
tled over by rival claimants, each pricked
with the spur of greed, and how the work of

an American author, if once, in the idiom of
the day, it "catches on," is nearly certain of
being denounced as a plagiarism and even
contested in the courts by some pickpocket
idler.

"I am afraid, however," Fabian continued, "that the mere production of my
play, with certain scenes and pages of dia-
logue preserved while others were either
reconstructed or quite left out, would not in
any real degree satisfy me. I should prefer,
indeed, to have the whole four acts of it fail
as I wrote them than succeed as you or anyone else might cleverly regarnish them.
And perhaps your mutilations might be tact
or acumen itself. Still, they would not be
my creations, the fruit of my reveries regarding certain theories, problems, doubts,
beliefs."

"I see," said Mr. Belsize, with a crest-
fallen manner. "But we can't bring the
play out as it is; we don't dare. And you,
Mr. Dimitry—excuse my telling you so, but
you're beating the sea with sticks. It's no
use treating American theatre-goers as if they

were very far above fools. They never have been, they probably never will be, and the times when I feel that truth most keenly are when I've just made a real hit with some fixed-up foreign play at the Academic. With all your skill in epigram, your lightness of literary touch and your knack at rounding off and emphasizing character, you should write a novel, for if you did so it would give you a blaze of renown."

"Is a blaze of renown so desirable?" said Fabian, and he laughed, and while he laughed Mr. Belsize recoiled politely, staring at him a little, as though he were an animal product not promptly to be classified. "I don't want renown at all," proceeded Fabian, most amiably and with utter candor. "I'd like my play to have it, though, if the world were willing."

"But you don't realize what the world is," cried his companion, with a touch of quaint entreaty. "The world, as regards the American theatre, is an ass. It can never grasp you; it can never feel you; you might go on writing those beautiful plays for it

through an eternity and it would pay you
back nothing but unconcern. Good heavens!
how does the New York populace go to the
theatre? For the purpose of being charmed
as if by a charming book? No. They hurry
there excited, nervous, to be more excited
and to be made more nervous. If it's drama
of even the good sort they want to quit the
theatre thrilled and harrowed. If it's comedy
of even the good sort they want to quit the
theatre tickled into a semi-hysteria. A fig, to
them, for your *nuances* and your *délicat-
esses!* They crop them up as a cow does a
daisy."

"Oh, very well," replied Fabian, who was
now a little weary. "You speak of my
writing novels. I've no cult for that kind
of attempt. Besides, it seems to me that
novels are flooding us. Everybody is making
them, and the wonder is that so many make
them as well as they do. If our age isn't
ready for this kind of effort I present, all the
worse that I should have tried to tax its
unripe developments. . . I don't see, Mr.
Belsize, that there's anything more to be said.

I'm not obstinate; I'm only convinced.
Kindly return me my manuscript, and I will
promise you and Mr. Lascelles to trouble
you both with no further scrolls of the same
impossible outlay."

Fabian left the Academic with his play in
his pocket, but by no means as hundreds of
poor authors have done when convinced
of managerial repulse. Starvation did not
stare him in the face, but a fact almost as
dreary did thus envisage him. He understood the utter hopelessness of trying. The
achievement of true dramatic fame seemed
visibly to lift and spread above him like the
dome of a monstrous cavern. He had no sense
of being crushed; his ambition was not
founded on vanity, as so often happens with
men of his aim and make, in whom cynic
revolt speaks like the *voix du sang* of a breed
fed on fare of caste and place.

" I suppose I shall always go on writing
plays," he said to himself, as he walked
homeward through the fitful gloom and
gleam of an April afternoon. " But such as
they are, they will not be worthy of the

Academic and of Mr. Belsize's wanton ma-
nipulations—Heaven forbid!"

He wondered, while thus musing, that no
despondency laid its touch on his spirits.
But soon the explanation grew sweetly yet
inexorably clear. He was going home to
recount his defeat. And to whom? To Alicia!

IX.

She was radiant with sympathy, and
Eninger as well. Fabian laughed at them
both for their vivid expressions of regret.

"I should hate," he said, "to see my play
emblazoned and filigreed into popularity. I
suppose every artist is at root an egotist, but
that does not of necessity make him a
mountebank. And after all, it matters very
little. I don't claim any great philosophic
sapience, but it has long ago seemed to me
that the sole unmercenary joy a man gets
from pen, brush or chisel is in simply wield-
ing either with patience and love. Human
applause, delicious though some ears find it,
never yet fully satisfied. It is always either
too loud, or not loud enough. No wonder that
wisdom often prefers the compromise of
silence."

"It's pleasant to feel that you are proof
against disappointment," said Alicia; and a

soft thrill passed through Fabian as she spoke the words. The realization of her sympathy was so exquisite to him that he would have braved severe disappointment for just the purpose of hearing a few such humane sentences from her lips. For he still loved her with inalienable passion, and there were times when the fever and tumult wrought in him by living as near her as he did, were a harsh challenge to endurance. Then again he would feel throes of the happiest gratitude for being thus vouchsafed an existence so entirely shorn of all former tedium, so freighted with pleasure that still deserved no other name, although its quality was both hectic and aggravating, and pain lay like a coiled worm at its core.

Eninger now devoted himself with great push and warmth to his profession, using what means of advancement were given him by the name he bore in this the city of his birth. Through the early weeks of spring he began to detect signs of increasing thrift. Several rich and important patients put themselves in his hands, half through luck and half because they had been friends of his parents, or of kindred more remote. He was glad, for this reason, that Fabian chose to accompany his wife in his own stead on little social pilgrimages which would sadly have tyrannized over his needed time. His faith in his wife's love for him had now become absolute. As regarded his thoughts about Fabian's feelings toward Alicia, these might have been named a nullity. He looked upon Fabian through spectacles ideally roseate. Even allowing that his friend still loved Alicia, how could there be a shadow of danger for her in the companionship of so splendidly self-controlled and moral a being? She was doubly guarded, in the first place by her wifely allegiance, and in the second by Fabian's almost saintly honor.

Eninger, let it here be said, was wholly right in his estimates. We know how sensitive was his nature to all shades of emotion, impression and conviction. He had not erred now; he knew what he was doing, or rather what he quietly waived the performance of. But a certain extraneous force presently strove to thrust sly stabs within the creases of his rather tough panoply.

He visited Mrs. Westerveldt morning after morning. He soon discovered that her neuralgia was merely a dainty myth and that she wanted his society—or at least had chosen to seem as if she wanted it—far more than any of his curative drugs. He had repeated twinges of conscience during these interviews, for the woman, in her perfect grace and her marble loveliness, fascinated him as he scarcely dared admit to himself. Through quite an interval she refrained from showing him any knowledge that Fabian, his wife's old lover, had become a resident in his home. Then, a little later, she contrived to make it appear as if he himself had informed her of this occurrence.

She always received him in gowns that were marvels of quiet taste. Her dwelling was modesty and luxury interblent in captivating comminglement. She said to him one morning, when the talk drifted upon charm in women and their modes of creating it:

"I can't think why it is that so many tellers of stories like to associate their feminine pets with 'a delicate perfume peculiar to herself,' or 'an odor of that undefined sort which clung to every fold of her garments,' or trash like that, of which we are forced to read pages and pages. The truth is, no woman who has the really cultured sense can endure that kind of atmospheric self-advertising. Show me one who is attended forever and a day by a 'soft, clinging perfume' which only she possesses, and I will both deny the originality of her bottle of scent and explain to you that she is a person of sleeping if not active vulgarities. A woman who is healthful and cleanly of life should always have the good sense to content herself with a drop or two of pure English cologne on her handkerchief. Essences are an infamy; they should only belong to the women who are not on my list of conversational topics."

He would watch her as she sat beside him, with her white, taper hands and her educated smile. It seemed to him that she was

the sort of woman to set nearly any man's
heart beating wildly, and yet somehow she
quite failed of this effect as regarded himself.
Perhaps it might have been wholly other-
wise but for the tender domination of Alicia's
influence. At the same time Gertrude Westerveldt charmed him. Only, her sway could
never pass beyond certain bounds. He wondered if she were beginning to detect this,
for it had occurred to him that she was bent
on some sort of conquest—on receiving some
sort of distinct surrender.

"What a blissful little family-group you
must make," she said, after he had been
adroitly lured, one morning, into a description
of the life they led in Forty-Second Street,
now that Fabian had gone there. "You send
shudders of envy through my poor solitary
soul."

"No state of human affairs could be very
blissful," replied Eninger, "with that old
Diogenes of a Colonel Delamere constantly
at his growls."

"He must be trying. And your wife can
not repress him?"

12

"I sometimes think a ball-and-chain couldn't."

"But after all, he is only a slight trial. You've so much else to be thankful for."

"Ah, now you're sneering."

"I?"

"Yes. You think this new arrangement a most extraordinary one."

She gracefully lifted both hands for a moment, and then dropped them. "But I don't sneer at extraordinary things. On the contrary, I sometimes delight in them."

"Oh, convention is a powerful god in your theogony," he said. "Don't assert that it isn't."

"I like what is called good form," she returned; "I like it in everything."

"And you don't consider it good form for Fabian Dimitry to have come to live with us?"

"Bless me, how you take a person up," she smiled. "Did I even suggest anything so rude? And surely it's altogether a question of how your wife stands the wear and tear."

"The wear and tear?" he echoed. And then, leaning back a little in his chair, he looked at her doubtfully, as though uncertain whether she were satiric or merely sportive. "In the name of common-sense," he went on, seriously and with even a tinge of pique, "you can't mean that I'm not sure of just the way in which my wife regards her past?"

"Common-sense has very little to do with matters of emotion," she said. "Don't appeal to it, for as a patron of sentiment it's a hollower god than the convention you accuse me of adoring."

He bit his lip; she irritated while she diverted him.

"It's no matter of emotion with Alicia," he asserted, somewhat crisply; "Fabian is her friend and mine. There everything begins—and ends."

He watched the coming of her cold little skeptical smile. He was prepared to see it dawn, chill and slight, at the tips of her lips. But when it came it vexed him, nevertheless.

"He was once her lover," she said, almost under her breath, and looking down while she lightly brushed some speck from the lap of her frock.

"I was once yours," he responded, with a daring born of his covert exasperation.

She lifted her eyes to his, and her smile grew bright, even ample, for her. "I haven't gone to live in Forty-Second Street," she murmured, with a sarcasm that seemed wrapped in soft veils of mirth. "I wonder how your Alicia would feel if I did go. Would she be uncomfortable? Ah, there would not exist for her any earthly reason. We were never engaged; we never plighted vows to each other. Besides, she has no doubt the same immense faith in you that you repose in her."

"A faith you reproach me for entertaining."

"Have I said that?"

"I shouldn't like to think that you disliked my wife."

"Disliked her? What conclusive leaps you take! She's a very enviable woman."

"Thanks. But that isn't saying that you like her."

"I admire her. I've not yet had the chance to become fond of her. *Ça marche*, however . . . we're getting to be better friends all the while. In the meantime I've reached one fixed belief about her."

"And that is?"

"She's a particularly clever woman. She has much more tact and shrewdness than I at first gave her credit for."

These latter tones of Mrs. Westerveldt's were more than innocently non-committal in their quiet ring. Eninger now rose and glanced at his watch, like the delayed physician he really was. Having taken his leave, shortly afterward, he began to feel, as he walked through the sunshine of a day rarely suave for New York in early March, that a little drop of poisonous alarm and discomfort had stolen into his being. But to meet Fabian once more and answer his honest gaze, brought stings of self-rebuke. He so utterly trusted his friend that this thought came to him: If Fabian himself believed there was any *arrière pensée* of a dangerous kind in Alicia he would never have con-

sented to take his recent step. Looking once
more into Alicia's eyes produced a like sense
of compunction.   He almost found himself
regretting that Mrs. Westerveldt had gra-
ciously agreed to come and dine at his house
on the following day.

But the dinner proved as pleasant as it
was informal.   The Colonel's bronchitis,
breaking out in a sudden severe attack and
keeping him upstairs aflame with anathemas
against the hateful American mutability of
the climate, produced an absence that only
hypocrisy could have mourned.   Mrs. Westerveldt appeared to lay aside her statelier
reserve as though it were an opera-cloak that
she had let slip from her neat-modelled
shoulders.   These shoulders were darkly
beclouded with the same black lace that
filmed itself over the sable silk of her gown,
and she wore no jewels except three or four
tiny clusters of diamonds glittering from the
region of throat and bosom.   She chose to
show how charmingly animated and affable
she could be at a small dinner like the present one, and after she had left the dining-

room with her hostess, Eninger and Fabian
discussed her quite admiringly over their
cigarettes.

Entering the drawing-room, they found
that neither Alicia nor her guest awaited
them there. Both ladies, as it happened,
were at this moment upstairs in Alicia's
dressing-room. They had seated themselves
beside one another on an inviting divan, near
a fire that sparkled cheerily in the shaded
light. For some little time they talked
together, and during these moments Mrs.
Westerveldt seemed clothed for her observer
in a wholly new mantle of fascination. She
had been delightful at dinner; up here she
became attractive in a fresh and even more
feminine way. She questioned Alicia about
her transatlantic life and yet with not the
least touch of what could seem undue curi-
osity. Was she putting forth, for some
reason, her full powers of enchantment? If
indeed there was any effort of this nature it
now passed wholly unperceived.

"How is it," she at length said, "that
you Englishwomen so often have such lovely

coloring! You must forgive me for being so personal, but there's a rose, just now, on either of your cheeks that seldom enough grows in our Western gardens."

Each rose turned a little redder, and Alicia laughed with a fluttered tone as she answered: "I'm a bit nervous this evening, somehow. I suppose that has made me look flushed."

Mrs. Westerveldt took her hand, caressing it with both her own. "I thought nobody was ever nervous in your country," she said. "I had supposed that we Americans monopolized nerves completely. Your hand is really quite hot. I hope you're never a victim, by the way, to my own horrid foe, neuralgia?"

"No," said Alicia. With a sudden gesture that seemed half unconscious, she drew away the hand that her companion held, and lifted it an instant toward the back of her head. "But I have strange darting pains *there*," she said, "though only at times."

"And you tell your husband about them?"

"No."

"And pray why not?"

"Oh, I hate to worry him. He's had annoyances enough, as it is, of late. We've both had."

"Ah, these may account for your pains. But I thought you were very happy. You have seemed very happy, always, though I admit that you do sometimes have a slightly worried look."

"I am happy —deeply so, as far as concerns *him.*"

"Him? Your husband, of course?"

"Who else?"

"Then there are other causes for your discontent? But I'll annul that question; I'll consider it unspoken; it sounds fatally familiar."

"Don't think it so," Alicia gently exclaimed. "Yes, there are other causes. It's almost a borrowing of trouble, however, for me to speak of them. Perhaps I should dismiss them altogether. Ray tells me I should —but never mind." She broke off here, with what seemed to her auditor an odd abruptness. Quickly afterward she rose. "Shall we go down-stairs again?" she asked.

"By all means, if you wish."

"Perhaps the gentlemen have ended their smoking."

"Yes; their tobacco is a dreadful tyranny, isn't it?" murmured Mrs. Westerveldt, as she moved toward the dressing-glass. "May I look at myself here for an instant?"

"Oh, by all means," Alicia answered. And just then her guest saw her stoop and pick up something, which flashed like an electric spark before she hid or seemed to hide it. This was witnessed in the mirror by Mrs. Westerveldt, and for a brief space not remarked as an act of the slightest import. But presently she was assailed by a sense of loss, glancing downward at the dark laces which clad her breast.

"Ah, too bad!" she said.

Alicia glided up to her. "What is too bad?" came her question.

"One of my little diamond stars must have dropped from my gown. I remember that the pin was slightly disjointed; my maid told me so this evening. Could I have lost it here?"

"Here?" replied Alicia. Mrs. Westerveldt turned and faced her as she thus spoke. Those roses on her cheeks had suddenly vanished.

"I'm very sorry," she went on, and began to search the carpet with drooped head. Mrs. Westerveldt stood and watched her while she did so. Presently the two searched together. "Shall I call a servant?" soon continued Alicia. "Or perhaps I'd better turn up all the lights."

"Thanks," replied Mrs. Westerveldt: "I mean, you may make it brighter if you will kindly do so. That is all."

Alicia went to the gas-fixtures and quickly filled the room with a much keener radiance. Then, under this new aid, the search recommenced. But meanwhile Mrs. Westerveldt's eyes had slipped certain covert glances toward the face of her hostess. Alicia's paleness appeared sharply unusual, and once or twice her step had almost the effect of a stagger.

"Oh, very well," Mrs. Westerveldt suddenly said, ceasing to scan the floor. "I should not be surprised if I had made some mistake."

"Some mistake?" faltered Alicia, meeting the gaze directed on her and then averting her eyes.

"Yes, Mrs. Eninger," came the answer, very softly and courteously uttered. "It's no doubt all my own stupidity. I dare say my maid did not give me the little star, after all. I'm so forgetful about these trifling matters. If I'm wrong, however, and you should come across it in dining-room, drawing-room, hall, or anywhere, please have the goodness—but I needn't ask *that*, need I?" And she smiled quite brilliantly upon Alicia, adding: "Now, pray do not bore yourself with thinking about this trifle for another moment . . . Let us go down and join the gentlemen, as you suggested."

"But I will order the servants—" began Alicia.

"Oh, no," amiably broke in Mrs. Westerveldt. "Pray do nothing of the sort. As I said, it may all have been the fault of my maid, who probably put the jewel back into my box . . . "

They went down-stairs soon afterward, but Mrs. Westerveldt, as they descended, managed to make some new arrangement of her small scintillant ornaments, thus rendering the gap caused by the missing one far less noticeable.

Alicia did not refer to the affair when the drawing-room was reached and Eninger and Fabian had been discovered there. Mrs. Westerveldt furtively waited, yet no reference came. She had already drawn her own conclusions; they soon grew more bitingly distinct. The chill of an actual horror had fallen upon her, but she tried to shake it off. In this her success was only partial; there were intervals when the voices of Fabian and Eninger sounded far away, as if they were calling to her from the next room. Why did not Alicia speak? It was damning, all things considered, that she should not . . . At last the hour for her departure had come. She rose and went up to Alicia, saying, "I've had a most delightful evening," with lips that seemed to her as if they must be blanched an ashen hue. But soon afterward, while giving a quick stare at herself in a long glass, she saw that her face had not altered. She was a woman who believed in being calm; perhaps Eninger would have judged more correctly of her if he could have known that she had had at least one emotion in her life, and that one—himself. But surely all other deep feeling had suffered in her a process of massacre, silent yet total. However, such repression and extinction may have been brought about is not by any means as easy for the analyst of the human heart to explain as for the astronomer to tell us how he weighs a world in space. One effort has behind it the lucid laws of mathematics; the other deals with a far more baffling infinity.

Fabian escorted her into her carriage. She was trembling, as he closed the door with a hollow little clash, from an agitation to which all her past life of serene self-equipoise proffered no parallel. She threw herself back on the cushions of the vehicle and with locked teeth groaned aloud.

"I loved that man, Ray Eninger," ran her

thoughts, as the wheels below her smote
strident on the stony avenue. "I loved
him, and I married another man for money
because my heart was weary and tortured.
Ah! how well I remember it all after these
years! . . . But now I find him the husband of a woman like that! A woman he
loves, and who dares to pose as one who
loves him in return. *She!* It's monstrous—
horrible! That turquoise ring I almost discharged my maid, Françoise, for stealing on
the night *she* dined with me . . . why,
who but *she* took it, standing there at my
dressing-table as she did? I never dreamed
of suspecting her then. But to-night—to-
night! . . . "

The carriage rolled on, with harsh clatters
that gradually grew like spoken words to
the ear on which they struck.

Mrs. Westerveldt had remained until now
the speechless prey of her own savage musings. But now she straightened her form in
the dusk, and with hands instinctively
clenched she spoke aloud what rang to her
own sense like the translation into clearer

phrase of those discords wrought by the driving vehicle:

"This Englishwoman he's married is a thief—a thief—a thief!"

When the carriage presently stopped at her own door she was so faint and unnerved that her footman had to give her his arm before she could alight and ascend the stoop.

X.

"I'm furious about the way the Academie has treated you," said Mrs. Atterbury one afternoon to Fabian, when he had dropped in for the purpose of telling her the news concerning his proffered play. "This Belsize is a horrid wretch; I've heard of him; he always wants a pot of money for lobbying American plays through the theatre."

"Oh, Belsize isn't so blamable," replied Fabian, almost gaily. "He's only the inevitable product of his time."

"He's an extortionist and a spendthrift," exclaimed the little lady. "Yes, he's both. I know him. I've heard all about him from three or four of my literary friends. He smokes the most expensive cigars; he drinks champagne like water; he's a luxurious Bohemian. And he has Mr. Lascelles under his thumb. There wasn't any earthly reason why he should have dared to propose your giving him that money."

13

"I would gladly have given it to him," said Fabian.

"You would, you goose!" cried Mrs. Atterbury. "Then why on earth *didn't* you?"

"Because I didn't feel like bribing him to leave the play alone and make believe to Mr. Lascelles that he'd wrought wonders with it."

"Oh, you *do* think him a fraud, then?"

"I dare say that few of us are intentional frauds."

Mrs. Atterbury pursed her lips and gave her head a cogitative slant. Then a characteristic answer came from her, made up of sound sense and flippancy in motley conjunction.

"I do so detest that exonerating style toward self-evident humbugs. We can pardon an ass if he talks sophistries. But when a clever rogue like this Belsize does it, he needs a knock-down fist, straight from the shoulder. Now, look here: your work has nature's own beauty and power in it; its tints and tones and lights are as true as one of Constable's best landscapes. You've got satire—lots;

but you've charity to counterbalance it, and
make just the proper harmony we mean by
that funny little misused word we call art.
You've got other qualities—oh, confound
it all, *I'm* not to be gammoned with the
sly rot of a special pleader like this fellow,
Belsize. He had his own axe to grind, and
thought you'd help him put a sharp edge on
it."

"And *you* thought," said Fabian, smiling,
"that I should have used that axe to hew
my path toward fame and fortune?"

She looked at him in her genuine, earnest,
slightly rowdy way. "Oh, stuff! I don't
believe you care a fig for either fame *or*
fortune! You'd keep writing your exquisite
plays if you'd been cast on a lonely island
and never expected to get off it." Here she
made a slight grimace. "But I don't know
about the solitude; I'm afraid you'd hate
that pretty badly for *one* reason. Your
Egeria couldn't be found in any of those
island grottoes, you know; she's a goddess
peculiar to Forty-Second Street."

"And one," he answered, rather sombrely,

"in whose divinity you seem to repose very little faith."

"I've not met her at all often, please remember. Personally, I've always thought her fetching to any degree."

"Who's fetching to any degree?" said a voice in the doorway, and Lewsy Atterbury, home from Wall Street a little earlier than was his wont, lounged into the room. "Show me a woman that's more fetching than my wife, and I'll send her the swellest landau that'll be seen in the park from now till next July."

"Good heavens, Lewsy," exclaimed Mrs. Atterbury; "as if she'd accept it unless she were frightfully bad form!"

"*Isn't* that a comfortable chair you've got?" proceeded Lewsy, as Fabian rose to shake hands with him. "'Pon my word, I don't believe there's a chair in this whole town that can quite match it. Just run your hand round among those side cushions—see how deep they are; how they sort of sneak into the small of your back and the rear part of your ribs. Eh? Isn't that true?" And then

he began a narration about his unique luck
in picking up the chair at a wondrously low
price. Fabian only half listened. Once he
had thought Lewsy a diverting egotist, but
of late his vaunts had appeared too steeped
in monotony.

"We were just talking about Mrs. Eninger, Lewsy," now said his wife, while Fabian
shot toward her a glance of involuntary dis-
approval. "*She's* a fetching woman. If
you don't think so you mustn't say it, or
you'll run the risk of being torn limb from
limb."

"Mrs. Eninger?" Lewsy seemed to muse.
"Oh, yes; she's a beauty—a stunning
beauty." He turned to Fabian with eyes
a-twinkle and visible laughter lurking below
his large moustache. "I'll bet, though, Dimitry, that she don't measure round the waist as
little as my Adela does. Now we both know
that Adela *is* a trifle stout for her size; but
then ——"

"Lewsy, do you want to be throttled, you
personal scamp, you?" cried Mrs. Atterbury.

Fabian felt a light wave of disgust sweep

through his nerves.   He no longer could see
the least trace of amusement in this coarse
boasting on the part of his friend's husband.
Mrs. Atterbury, perhaps discerning his annoyance, chose to pull a sharp rein upon her
frivolities.   Abruptly she became decorous,
demure, thoughtful.   She showed Fabian
that side of her individuality which in certain moods he had almost grown to cherish.
The change in her seemed quick as if magic
had made it.   On a sudden, as it were, he
heard her saying:

. : . "Oh, yes; my Wednesdays *are* a
social failure, and the more I see of New
York the more I realize the impossibility of
a *salon*.   There's a real pathos in the way
caste deports itself here.   It has none of the
self-reliance that belongs to aristocracies
oversea.   It's afraid of its own respecta-
bility; it doesn't dare unbend.   Mrs. Amsterdam comes to drawing-rooms and looks all
about her with a little provincial simper that
I've learned to know by heart.   She'd love to
plunge into things and have a good frank talk
with Jones, the journalist, or **Tamarini**, the

tenor. But she's a mortal inward dread that to do so might hurt her escutcheon of rank—orig inally a sign-board over some little shop near the Battery, where her ancestors, only a few generations ago, vended anything at retail, from tobacco to cutlery. . . No, I despair of trying ever to make sets mix. Large civilizations do that. London does it very successfully; Paris does it as only Paris can; New York will some day do it, but by that time I suppose they'll be reading our names on the tombstones at Greenwood Cemetery and wondering what a village New York must have looked like when Central Park was considered up town and High Bridge was actually called a suburb."

Fabian broke into a pleased smile at this; he had, in a way, got his old friend entertainingly and suggestively back again. But in a trice Lewsy spoiled everything for him by an affable slap on the thigh and a gleeful exclamation of——

"*There*, old chap! How's that for a burst of wit and wisdom combined and condensed . . eh? D'you believe Mrs. Eninger could

beat it! I guess she'd have to get up pretty
early in the morning if she wanted to."

Fabian found a prompt opportunity of
taking his leave. Just before he did so he
told his hostess that perhaps he might accompany Mrs. Eninger to her next Wednesday,
but that he thought Mr. Eninger had an engagement for that particular evening. After
he had gone, Lewsy returned from having
seen their guest out at the hall-door, and
joined his incomparable Adela, with a long,
significant whistle.

"So, Ad, eh, it's come to this, has it?" he
drawled, in a nasal exaggeration doubtless
caught from Wall Street.

"What do you mean, Lewsy?" said his
wife, with a kind of absent tartness in her
tone.

"So Dimitry's beginning to drop into
Eninger's shoes, is he?"

"Hush, please."

"At present he wears them now and then,
just for a flyer. Pretty soon he'll want to
wear them altogether. Isn't that about the
size of it?"

"Oh, nonsense. Recollect he might have married her once, if he'd felt inclined."

But even while Mrs. Atterbury thus spoke, the current of her thoughts took a different turn. She had begun to distrust Alicia, and with severer bitterness than she herself knew. The conviction that Ray Eninger's wife was all art and subtlety in her dealings with Fabian had become matter for incessant concern. Yes, Alicia was doubtless as deep as the sea—what else did the whole affair look like? She had two men at her beck and call; she was playing a game that some women loved better than to wear a new dress every day in the year. She was one of your seeming-innocent coquettes, who hid the wisdom of a serpent inside the coo of a dove. "It might have been luckier for Fabian Dimitry," Mrs. Atterbury would sometimes muse, "if he'd married her and she'd borne him mad children. Now he's gone back to sit at her feet, and suffer. He won't grant that he's not having a glorious time. Still, I can read, as it were, between the lines of his life."

All this while Mrs. Atterbury was not really sure if her doubts were justified. She wanted to see more of Alicia, and at her own reception the following night she made a decided point of doing so. Alicia came with Fabian, her beauty and grace attracting instant attention as she entered the room, and causing several gentlemen for whom Mrs. Atterbury's rather promiscuous Wednesdays meant their sole excursions into the *grand monde*, promptly to seek introductions. It stung his hostess as she observed how Fabian hovered always in the wake of Alicia. There were at least five or six ladies in the rooms to whom he had been presented, but he either forgot this fact or ignored it. His vassalage was in both cases, however, equally irritating. Mrs. Atterbury watched it and grew almost alarmed at the secret turmoil it stirred in her. But for this effect she had a speedy mental explanation—or believed that she had. Women who stand, as she did, on the borderland of passion, are apt to tell themselves that the tropic air they breathe into their nostrils has got its warmth from friendship alone.

Her rooms were somewhat more crowded
to-night than usual. "You see," she said
to Alicia, "there's a strong tincture of the
Four Hundred here besides my unfashion-
able friends. It's Lent, you know, and some
of the smart people have nothing better to
do than come to *me*."

But she contrived, nevertheless, to stand
for a good while at the elbow of Eninger's
wife, and finally, as if with an idea of quite
taking the young Englishwoman unto herself,
she slipped her arm within Alicia's and murmured something that Fabian failed to over-
hear. But he followed in the wake of the two
ladies as they pushed politely through the
throng, and at last paused before a closed
door, after having traversed more than one
festal room. Then Mrs. Atterbury turned
and perceived him, and at once she said,
with a hardness in her voice but no incivility:

"Oh, it's you, is it? I was going to show
Mrs. Eninger my Lewsy's collection. You've
seen it, I believe."

"Yes; more than once," replied Fabian,
plainly unsuspicious of the truth.

Mrs. Atterbury opened the door and disclosed an interior much smaller than either of the rooms just crossed. She detested seals, cameos, etc., when viewed purely from the collector's point of view, and so did her husband, who would never have brought together the present cabinetful. It had been bequeathed him by an uncle who had passed many years in the rôle of the rich American virtuoso living abroad; it was of dark, reddish wood, exquisitely carved, and it rose against the rich-tinted wall of the little chamber dedicated to it, with a delicate antique dignity.

"If ever a man had a white elephant on his hands," declared Mrs. Atterbury, after she had shut the door beyond which they had all three passed, " it is my poor Lewsy in his possession of this cabinet." She flitted to a corner and reached her short arm ludicrously down into the interior of a huge Japanese vase. " We keep the key here, in the most reckless way," she proceeded. "It's flinging temptation into the teeth of our servants, as I often tell Lewsy. But then

we're both so careless about keys and things
like that . . . Ah, there it is; I've nearly
broken my arm trying to get it."

At once the cabinet was opened, and many
small, beautiful treasures were disclosed.
Mrs. Atterbury, in her most flippant mood,
began to rattle nonsense about the worth of
the superb collection, and her frequent long-
ings to spend it as if it were a practicable
bank-account. Fabian, who had some knowledge of such gems, though slight cult for
them when ranged in rows after this museum-
like fashion, regarded them now for the third
or fourth time with relative indifference.
He was perhaps too preoccupied to notice
that Mrs. Atterbury secretly bristled with
annoyance. She had wanted a private talk
with Alicia, a talk of exploit, study, acute
observation. His presence had possibly never
before been distasteful to her. But it was
because of him that she really wished, just
then, to have him absent from the wife of his
friend.

Alicia bent over the rarity and riches of
the collection with eyes that pleasurably

glistened.   For a little while Mrs. Atterbury
spoke in a light, explanatory, brilliant manner of this or that jewel, hinting at historic
and archaic details which few but her inti-
mates might have accredited her with pos-
sessing.   Then, while Alicia continued her
scrutinies, with golden head picturesquely
bowed, the lady of the house turned toward
Fabian.   It so chanced that over the low,
plump shoulder of Mrs. Atterbury Fabian
could plainly see Alicia's profile, the droop
of her graceful arms, the movement or repose
of her slender hands.

"By the way," said his hostess, "I saw
they're advertising a new play as 'in prepara-
tion' at the Academic."

"Yes, I saw," said Fabian.

"Something from the German, this time,
revised and adapted by your friend, Mr. Belsize."   Mrs. Atterbury spoke the name with
a mutinous curl of her lip.   "Oh, what a
race of snobs we Americans are in all matters
of art!   How afraid we are to come out
honestly and cultivate the works of our own
countrymen!   It's bad enough with our

dramatists, but at this hour and in this town we've American painters of genius almost without bread to give their wives and children. . . What! are you so surprised to hear it?"

"No—no," replied Fabian quickly, "not surprised at all." He had been looking at Alicia, for a few seconds, and it would appear as if something he had seen her do had driven the color from his cheeks in this dismayed style. Mrs. Atterbury stared at him rather bewilderedly, and then turned toward Alicia, who had just quitted the cabinet.

"Have you finished your inspection?" she asked. "And has it really not bored you?"

"Oh, one could go on looking all night," was the answer.

"You may do so if you please," laughed Mrs. Atterbury. "I'll send you in a quart or two of *bouillon*, and Mr. Dimitry will of course remain and keep you company."

The intended satire was wholly lost upon Fabian. His eyes were fascinated by the face of Alicia, and if they did not brim with wild alarm it was because of the self-control he had swiftly exerted. Alicia did not respond to his look. He saw that a slight new flush had come into her cheeks and that her lips were in a faint tremor. Mrs. Atterbury had meanwhile gone to the cabinet for the purpose of closing and locking it.

Suddenly she started back. "Why, what is this?" she exclaimed.

No one spoke. Alicia did not; Fabian could not. Mrs. Atterbury's gaze went from his face to hers. It paused at the latter before transferring itself back to the gap she had just discovered in a certain row of the neat-ranged curios.

"Have you been playing a little practical joke upon me, Mrs. Eninger?" she asked.

"I?" faltered Alicia.

She smiled and put her head dubiously on one side. "Come, now. If you've just done it to frighten me, I'll forgive you." And she held out her hand toward Alicia.

Fabian found a voice, then. He addressed Alicia. "Mrs. Atterbury thinks, evidently, that you've reason to be forgiven." He tried to speak in careless tones, but wondered whether they really sounded as odd and hollow as his own ears reported them.

Alicia recoiled a little, with hands clasped together and blue eyes excitedly shining.

"I—I don't understand," she said. "What is it that you think I have done?"

Mrs. Atterbury's expression underwent an instant change. She hurried toward Alicia and laid a hand on each of her shoulders. "Oh, forgive *me!*" she broke forth. "I thought you might have taken one of the seals, but only in fun, of course. I'm so sorry if I've annoyed you!" She now darted to the cabinet once more. "Ah, what a pity, what a pity!" she cried. "This comes of Lewsy's carelessness and my own. One of the servants must have found out where we put that key. And yet I thought all our servants were such honest creatures. I thought——"

She came to a dead stop, then, and a blank look settled upon her face, like the blur of frost on a window-pane. She

14

knitted her brows in a perplexed way and lifted one hand to her forehead. "But I remember!" she at length cried, and pointed toward the spot marked by the absence of the missing gem. "It was there but a few minutes ago," she pursued, "when I first opened the cabinet. Yes—yes; I *can not* be mistaken. It was that amethyst intaglio, with the head of Hermes—almost the best thing here. I'm fond of it; I always notice it first, and I'd no sooner opened the cabinet this evening than I . . ."

But here she again paused. "Oh, what am I saying?" she speedily recommenced, but in a voice full of pained entreaty. "Don't think I mean any insult to—to either of *yourselves*. But I *saw* the amethyst, and—and how *could* it have been swept away by a sleeve or anything like that? They're all bedded so firmly in the velvet, and they're set too far back to be displaced by any such accident."

She was now busied in an eager survey of the collection. Her glance swept and reswept its various files. Then, with a

despairing shake of the head, she briefly
examined the underlying floor.

While this went on, Fabian had absorbed
himself in Alicia. She had let her form
drop into a chair, and sat with gaze riveted
on the carpet. It was carpet of a light pearl
color, and the whole apartment was so
bright-lit that almost any meagre speck
could have been discerned there.

Fabian drew near to her. He felt as if his
heart stood still, while he leaned down a
little and prepared to murmur a few words
in her ear. But just then Mrs. Atterbury
discontinued her search and whisked sharply
about, facing them both.

"Oh, if it's gone it's gone," she said, with
troublous and petulant accent. Her eyes
met Fabian's. "I'm so certain that I saw
it just now," she continued. "I——"

And at this point Fabian took several steps
toward her, with a quiet gesture that had
in it the force of veto.

"I have not contradicted you," he said,
"but I must do so now. You state that you
are sure you saw no empty place yonder—

that you saw a certain gem where the gap is now. Suppose I tell you that you're quite wrong."

"Wrong!" repeated Mrs. Atterbury, with a dazed mien.

"Yes," he proceeded. "*I noticed* that same empty interval a second or two after you had opened the cabinet."

Here Alicia lifted her head.

"You noticed it?" fell from Mrs. Atterbury. "Why, how strange! But no; no! I'm positive——"

"Ah, my dear lady," broke in Fabian, "I am positive as well." He gave a slight laugh, and she to whom he spoke started at it. "I've no wish to act uncivilly—you may or may not have taken the initiative there. But I repeat to you that I saw the void place which you declare was filled. Yes, I saw it," he added, more slowly, and with profound apparent meaning.

Silence followed. In the distance, from behind the closed door, sounded a babble of voices. Then the plaintive wail of a violin pierced these and silenced them.

"Albertini is beginning," said Mrs. Atterbury, with flurried vehemence. "And that Lewsy of mine is so apt to botch things when he plays master of ceremonies." At once she relocked the cabinet, slipped its key into her pocket, and hastened toward the door. There she remained motionless for a few seconds, and as if absorbed in meditation. " Well," she suddenly burst forth to Fabian, "I suppose you *are* right. You *must* be, of course. I showed the collection this morning to a little party of friends, and perhaps I confuse, in spite of myself, then with now. But that doesn't make the loss any less mysterious a one, does it? And . . . I—I do hope you'll both excuse me if, without intention, I have said the least thing that might have caused you . . . annoyance."

Fabian watched her look wander to Alicia as she spoke these apologetic words. He knew Adela Atterbury so well that he could now detect an unfamiliar spark in her eyes and note in her voice a complete lack of the truly repentant ring.

Alicia had risen, and before Fabian could

speak she said, in her dulcet voice and with entire repose:

"How could you have caused us annoyance, my dear Mrs. Atterbury? I saw that empty place, too, and we are both so sorry for you. . . Are we not?" and she turned to Fabian.

"Thanks," Mrs. Atterbury replied. The word was mechanic and cold to the ears of her friend, whatever Alicia's may have found it. "I'll see you again quite soon, I hope," she continued, in a voice of heartier inflection. And then she disappeared, leaving the door ajar.

Fabian and Alicia were left alone together. He went toward the door and caught hold of its knob. As he reclosed the door, Alicia exclaimed: "Why, what are you doing? Shall we not go out and hear the music?"

Fabian stared into her face, feeling his lips twitch a little. His hand fell from the knob. He seemed to hear within his brain the rapid and muffled beatings of his own heart.

"Have you nothing to say to me?" he asked.

"I?" murmured Alicia. She returned his gaze, with surprise and perhaps a little touch of arrogance. Then she slightly lifted her shoulders, and added: "No."

"In that case," answered Fabian, "I have something which I must say to *you*."

"What is it?" she asked. He had drawn quite close to her, and a sparkle was in his eyes that seemed as if wrath had kindled it there.

XI.

The way in which she faced him almost made Fabian recoil; she appeared so firmly self-possessed.

"I wished to tell you——" he began.

"Of what?" she inquired, with a high, scornful note in her sweet voice. "Of that woman's ill-breeding? I felt it, and no doubt you did as well. But probably she did not mean real rudeness. Her apology, I suppose, must be taken for what it is worth. . . Let us go into the drawing-rooms and hear the violinist. I am so fond of that sort of music when it is good, and even at this distance his sounds as if it were excellent."

Fabian gnawed his lip. Twenty different phrases occurred to him, but he could not put one of them into speech. Presently he said, with a repression of manner that he felt she must observe and weigh, knowing him as well as she did:

"Very well; I will accompany you. He

moved toward the door, she following. On
a sudden he reeled, like a man whose brain
has been beset by a blood-rush.

"You're ill!" cried Alicia, springing
toward him and laying a hand on his arm.

"No," he replied. Immediately he had
become like his usual self. He opened the
door and they went out together. As Alicia
crossed the threshold he heard her say:

"I don't think I'll care to stop much
longer. Our carriage was ordered for eleven,
wasn't it?"

"Yes."

"It's nearly that now, is it not?"

"It's after eleven."

"Then we'll go in about five minutes, if
you don't object. Do you?"

"Not at all."

The playing of Signor Albertini was fine,
and it lasted (including the rapturous *encore*
which he received) not more than six or
seven minutes in all. He was an artist com-
pounded of a certain laziness and a certain
ambition. The result caused him to measure,
at amateur performances, the patience of his

auditors, and always to leave it discreetly within the margin of weariness. As his last strains died away, Alicia turned to Fabian and quietly said:

"Let us go now. You see, Mrs. Atterbury is busy in conversation over yonder. Do not let us disturb her with our goodnights. Come." . . .

They had been several minutes in the carriage which drove them home, before the silence between them was broken. Then Fabian broke it.

"You thought Mrs. Atterbury rude?" he began.

"Yes; horridly . . didn't you?"

"She missed one of her cameos."

"True. But you told her——" And then Alicia ceased to speak. They sat opposite each other, but could not see one another's faces.

"I told her that she had made a blunder," Fabian said.

"In so many words—yes."

"Was I right?" While he put this question he felt every nerve in his body to be tensely strung as the chords of some instrument which another turn of the key might shatter into incompetence.

"Right!" came Alicia's answer, with a querulous ring. "Why, you said you saw that one of the gems was missing. How could you not have been 'right' if you told her that?"

Fabian threw back his head in the obscurity and sat thus with close-pressed lips.

And now there swept through the fibres of his brain just that change which for a man circumstanced like himself was perhaps the inevitable one. He found that extenuation was dipping for him in deep wells, and like a drinker hotly athirst he took the proffered draughts.

How, after all, if he had been tricked by some mere cheat of eyesight? Good heavens, had he really seen Alicia snatch that amethyst from the velvet shelf? Suppose he had been deluded by his own senses. Then how keen the insult, how monstrous the injustice!

Their carriage stopped; the drive had been but a short one. Fabian opened the door and sprang out. As Alicia gave him her hand he perceived that it was trembling terribly.

"I—I am afraid I shall fall," came her voice, feebler than he had ever yet heard it. But even then she made the effort to alight, and in doing so literally fell into his arms.

He almost bore her up the stoop. It soon was plain that she had nearly lost consciousness. Eninger, having heard the carriage stop, met them on the threshold.

Alicia's fainting state was a sharp shock to him. He seized her from the embrace of Fabian with gestures unconsciously austere. To lay her on a sofa in the near drawing-room was to discover that she had really swooned.

"What has caused this?" the husband questioned of his friend, with an imperiousness which doubtless he himself did not realize.

"I can not say," replied Fabian. "I had no idea she was ill until the carriage stopped —until I myself had left it."

Eninger was too good a physician not quickly to decide that the attack missed being serious. Before there was time to apply any restorative, Alicia unclosed her eyes. She did so with a look of affright, a hysterical scream, and a burst of tears.

"It is nothing," said Eninger to Fabian. "You had best leave us here together. I'll do what I can to quiet her."

Speaking thus, he momentarily turned his back upon his wife. Whatever she may now have effected in the way of a soothing discovery, her demeanor swiftly became calm. As Fabian quitted the room, she rose from the sofa.

"I think I will go up-stairs, Ray," she said. "I'll ring for Margaret to undress me."

"My darling," he softly cried, wrapping his arms about her; "how *did* it happen?"

"I don't know . . it came like a flash."

"You had not been dancing?"

"No."

"You were talking there in the carriage with Fabian?"

"Yes, Ray. . . Let me go up at once, won't you please, dear?"

"Of course . . this instant."

The next morning, as Fabian came down to
breakfast, he found Alicia seated at the
coffee-urn with no change for the worse on
her fresh-tinted face. The Colonel had just
begun a tirade which Eninger heard with his
usual saintly patience. It was à propos of
a wedding-invitation which had just been
courteously sent him by the mother of the
prospective bride, a certain Mrs. Van Wagenen, whom he had met once or twice under
his son-in-law's roof.

"So her daughter's going to marry the
Honorable Cecil Verrinder, is she — the
younger son of Lord Brecknock? Bless my
soul, it's an outrage the way these American
girls fly at the throats of our English boys!"

"It may be the other way," hazarded
Eninger carelessly, while buttering a bit of
toast. "Miss Eva Van Wagenen is worth one
million of money and she's the heiress to
another."

"Ah," said the Colonel, with an unholy
sourness on his lean visage. "Quite so, my
dear Ray. The Honorable Cecil sells his ped-
igree and position. Miss Van . . . I never

can either recollect or pronounce half your
jaw-breaking Knickerbocker names . . . Miss
Van Hodgepodge completes her pretty bar-
gain and gets a social grip on the Prince of
Wales's coat-tails forever and a day. How
nobly American! How magnificently repub-
lican! Who dares to call democracy a failure! .
'Gad, not I; I'm too afraid of having a head
put on me by some of these mighty Western
patriots. Isn't that the right phrase for one
to use, by the way . . . a head put on one?"
And the Colonel slipped his little silver egg-
spoon into the yellow heart of his already
decapitated egg.

Fabian just then took his seat at the table,
and Alicia, with an evident desire to miti-
gate the awkward pause (although her voice
did not seem to the new-comer by any means
her native and authentic one) here suavely
observed:

"Oh, well, father, you'll go and see Miss
Van Wagenen internationally married, I
hope, notwithstanding your dislike of his
bride's cold-blooded creeds."

"Spare poor Eva," said Eninger, with

gentle protest. "I knew her in pina-
fores. I dare say she's most genuinely in
love."

This gave the Colonel another opportunity
of being acrid; but all his three auditors
were already resigned to the fact that a ces-
sation of his bronchitis predetermined an
unpleasant breakfast-table.

Nobody appeared specially to remark his
new outbursts of airy venom. . . Fabian,
this morning, was unwontedly speechless,
though often he had his fits of silence—
always of a sort, though, which somehow
implied his quenchless amiability.

Near the door of his office Eninger turned
and saw his wife. "You're truly feeling
brighter?" he asked, and with a swift little
swerve of the hand his fingers were on her
pulse. She waited compliantly, for a few
seconds; and then he said: "You've taken
that medicine I gave you?"

"Yes."

"Well; remember the time for taking it.
You don't forget? No? I wouldn't go out
for three or four hours."

"But you're going out soon, I suppose."
And she touched his hair caressingly.

"Yes. . . But I'll see you at luncheon."

She suddenly looked about her, as if to make sure that the hall in which they stood was quite empty. Then she kissed him on the lips. Eninger did not like the kiss, deeply as he adored his wife. Her lips felt too feverish. . .

Going alone, a little later, into his office, he was soon joined by Fabian.

"Do you think she is unwell?" asked the latter, standing at his friend's side while Eninger sat before his desk.

"No. . . no," replied Alicia's husband. But he rose with a vague show of anxiety the next instant. Abruptly he grasped Fabian's hand.

"My dear boy!" he said . . and then he paused.

"Well?" responded Fabian.

Eninger laughed in a dashed way.

"I was a little brusque with you last night, was I not? I mean, when she fainted

like that. Did you notice it? Forgive me
if you did."

" Oh, readily, Ray. It was nothing. I—I
was worried about her."

" You're not worried now?"

" No . . yes."

" Yes?"

"I don't see why her pulse flutters so.
Her heart is as sound as a dollar. . . Well,
we doctors are the most empirical lot; what
do we really know? Are you going for a
walk? I shall go for a professional one in a
few minutes. . . . "

The first stopping-place Eninger made was
at Mrs. Westerveldt's. He had not seen
her since the evening of the dinner in his
own house, when she had appeared as the
single guest. He knew that she had expected
him quite a while ago. She received him
with one of her smiles, vague, characteristic;
he had not yet just made up his mind which
one it was when she had motioned him into
a seat and sank with feather-like pliancy
into another.

They talked for a while about her health,

until the subject became to Eninger ludicrous, and he forbore queries. He said a few things (rather aimless things, as he believed them) and then his patient somewhat pointedly inquired:

"And so your wife has been ill? That is too bad. And she got her trouble at the Atterburys'? Well, *there's* no vast matter for surprise."

"How you hate your stout little kinswoman."

She took no notice of this observation. "It was after driving home in the carriage with Mr. Dimitry? How unfortunate!"

"Unfortunate?" Eninger repeated.

"Oh, yes. I mean, that it should have happened there." He understood her smile, now, and disliked it; he had seen it before. "And your Fabian . . your dear friend . . he was the soul of devotion, naturally."

Eninger ground his teeth, and the anger flew redly to his cheeks. He tried to be tranquil, with some answer murderously ironic, and failed.

"I thought you disliked my wife," he

said, "and now I perceive that you wish to cast insult on her."

Those few ireful words had a knell in them for the woman who listened. They told her how this man loved his wife—how cold he was to her, Gertrude Westerveldt, and how he must so remain, as regarded all future powers of passion. They struck on her strange soul with the force of a tenfold slur. She at once spoke.

"I've cast no insult upon her," she said. "I should not know how to do so if I tried. What would be insult to a woman like that?" She rose, the next instant. "Come, now," she said, "tell me how it happened that you ever married such a creature?"

Her words appalled Eninger. He sprang erect, with clenched hands. "How dare you?" he exclaimed.

"I dare do much," came the answer, "when I see a man of your mind and strength so duped and fooled."

"Ah," he cried, "you are hideously cruel. This is the merest vulgar hate, spite, brutality. I will not listen to another word

from you. I should despise myself if I
did."

She had almost lost her head—she who had
kept it so coolly thus far throughout her
lifetime. His loyalty was like a venomed
barb to her. The thought seemed trebly
odious that he should taunt her with this
loyalty when its object was so despicable.
For since a certain evening there had been
nothing too bad that she could mentally call
Alicia. She had made up her mind that
Eninger's wife was the incarnation of all
human grossness. This conclusion was in
part due to her jealousy and in part to her
late experience. "A thief, a thief," kept
now ringing through her brain, as it had
rung for many a past hour. "A thief for
him, for Fabian Dimitry, her old lover,
whom she has got into the home of her
husband," rang there also, with haunting
and horrible cadence. She had meant to tell
Eninger just what she believed as certainty
regarding his wife. But now his sudden
declaration of departure stirred her with a
harsh dismay.

Her lips felt dry and hard as she sought
to use them. Eninger was at the threshold
of her room when she exclaimed:

"You speak of despising yourself. Despise *her!*"

Eninger raised his hand and shook it
toward the speaker with an expression of
blended indignation and pain. Then he
passed from the room.

Gertrude Westerveldt drooped her head
and brooded, with the sense of a poignard
fleshed and rusting in her bosom.

"How he loves that wretch!" she thought.
"And I did not tell him. I meant to tell him,
but I did not. . . She is a thief, but *why?*
Can it be for *him?* Dimitry has always
had money, and that legacy just left him
adds to it. . . Ah, well, she wants her
gains for herself. A woman who would do
the thing I saw her do—what vile purpose
may not sway her?"

Alone, sitting there in her home of wealth
and ease, this proud creature whom no one
had ever seen shed a tear, now bent her head
with an instinctive desire to hide the scalding

drops that burnt her cheeks while they fell.
But the tears had scarcely gushed from a
human source. Their heat had in it the sav-
agery of defeated passion.

Fabian went out into the streets almost
immediately after breakfast. The day was
chill but not inclement. He wandered up
town and down town. He was bitterly ill
at ease. Passing the Academic, he saw that
a fresh bill was announced for that evening.
Surprised at first, he remembered that he had
seen in some newspaper the statement that a
new play would be produced at this theatre
—an adaptation from the French by Mr.
Belsize—owing to the failure of a previous
production. He bought an orchestra-seat at
the box-office of the Academic and resolved
that he would not go back to Forty-Second
Street until bed-time. He went to see an
artist who was a friend of his, and sat for
two hours in a studio where several un-
sold and unsalable masterpieces gleamed as
rebukes to American taste and patriotism.
The artist was a genius, but neither explosive

nor misanthropic. He painted sturdily and did not jar his nerves by shrieks against his land and time. Fabian left him with a sense that there were many other spirits in the world as sorely lashed by fate as himself. It was not a new realization, but it somehow came to him, just now, fraught with a novel comfort.

After that he lunched frugally somewhere, with a languid appetite, and took another long walk, which ended at the door of Mrs. Atterbury.

She received him in bonnet and street-dress. "I had feared you were going abroad this pleasant day, or had already gone," he said, while she gave him her hand.

"No; I'm still at home, as you see. That is, I'm at home to you. There's hardly anyone else whom I would have seen just now."

"That's both frank and genial."

"I'm afraid I don't want it to be genial."

"You're in a bad humor?"

"Horribly."

"I suppose it has a definite cause," said

Fabian, slapping one knee with the limp fingers of his glove and keeping his look lowered while he did so.

Mrs. Atterbury's eyes were meanwhile fixed intently on his face. "Can't you guess the cause?" she said, and her voice was vibrant as if with hidden feeling.

"The loss of that precious intaglio?" These words Fabian spoke almost below his breath, while still not lifting his look.

"Yes and no," she answered, and her words now seemed to wear edges like a knife's and to cut the air of the room. "The mere loss of the seal was one thing: *how* its loss occurred was another."

Fabian did lift his look, then. "You haven't solved the mystery?" he asked.

"No—if it is one."

"Your answer is puzzling. Either there is a mystery or there is not."

She replied to him in tones more measured. "The statement *you* made, if made truthfully, of course creates a very dense mystery indeed."

He fired, at this, as she had perhaps

expected him to do. "So you suspect me of falsehood?" he demanded. Then, as she offered no response, he continued: "I doubt if there's a servant in your house who doesn't know just where the key of that cabinet is kept."

A smile, that seemed to him full of irony, flitted over her face. "Oh, good heavens!" she broke out, with what some people would have called her most vulgar manner but which was to him simply her most sincere one, "you're a fine dramatist, as I've told you many a time, but you're a very bad actor. I see it now; I wasn't ever sure of it before, because I've only known you when you were yourself."

He kept silent for a few seconds, with one foot making rapid little motions and both hands nervously pulling at the heavy fringe of a table-cloth close beside him. "Do you know," he presently began, "that you're accusing me of . . of hypocrisy?" (His eyes avoided hers, and his speech grew more hesitant as he went on.) "Do you realize that you're—you're placing me in . . well, in a position that . . that is quite horrible?"

"I don't place you in it. You place your-self in it."

"How! how!" he swiftly questioned, and caught up the gloves which he had thrown aside, almost seeming to tear them between his working fingers. "Don't you think I told you the truth last night when I said . . what . . I said?"

"No. You've hit the nail on the head precisely. I don't think you did tell the truth. I think you tried to ——"

She paused there, and a long, steadfast glance was exchanged between them.

Fabian put up one hand warningly; he had grown pale to the lips. "Be careful," he said.

She shrugged her shoulders and tossed her head. "My servants *didn't* know where that key was; I'll swear they didn't. . . I've been brooding over this whole matter. I can't *help* feeling as I do. . . Ah, do you know *why?*" she went on, with a wrath that drew down the lines of her mouth and clouded her brows. "The reason is this: reflection has convinced me that I *did* see

the amethyst there when I first opened
that cabinet. I'm fond of that one stone,
and somehow my eyes always light on it
first when I show the collection. I've really
loved it; only the other day I asked Lewsy
to let me wear it for a pendant on my diamond necklace. *I saw it*, do you understand." She leaned toward him fiercely,
and smote the table with one plump, clenched
hand. "If there's a man on God's earth,
Fabian Dimitry, whose word I'd believe
through thick and thin, that man is you.
But even such a man as you will lie for a
woman he's gone mad about."

Fabian rose; he was trembling. "You
believe I lied last night?" he asked.

"To shield her—yes."

"To . . shield her . . from what?"

"The charge of theft." And then Mrs.
Atterbury rose too.

"You must be mad," he said, his tones
husky and forced. "Theft? What conceiv-
able motive could that lovely and refined
creature have had in taking the stone?"

"Never mind her motive!" shot from his

hearer. "Still, she's grown poor, lately—or her husband has. It's frightful to say such words as these. I've never breathed a syllable of what I'm now saying. I've kept the least hint of it from Lewsy. I expected. you here to-day. Listen: this bonnet and walking-suit are both a sham. I'd lots of things to do, but I dare say I'd have staid in till dark, because when you come to me afternoon is usually your time. You did come, and you came to try and throw new dust in my eyes. Yes . . it's just that. *You saw her take the amethyst.* Oh, you'll deny it. I'm prepared to hear you deny it. You worship her, though you gave her up over there in London. Now you're at her feet. Mind, I don't breathe a ghost of a charge against *your* honor. That I know to be stainless—unstainable. But you're so much her slave that with all your truth and nobility you'd go straight into the jaws of hell if she called you there."

Dead silence now ensued between the speakers. Fabian's face was like marble. He walked toward the door, stopping within a slight distance of it.

"You are outrageous," he said, very collectedly. "I did not lie to you. I spoke the absolute truth. Alicia Eninger is the wife of my dearest friend. You heap infamy upon her, and expect me to endure such terrible charges. I've heard them calmly. If you were a man, I'd call you to account for them. You're a woman, and so I shall try to pity you."

He felt dizzy after he had got from the house into the street. He had never dreamed it possible that he could be called upon to defend Alicia in this fashion, whatever idea he might have had that inherited madness in her would take quaint and repugnant forms. But his recent defense now seemed to him clad with justice. Why not! He had never seen her really commit this act, nor had Mrs. Atterbury, either. He had lied to blunt the suspicions formed and cherished against her, and in all his life he could not remember having ever deliberately lied until now. But conscience did not smite him. He felt a deep resentment toward the woman he had just left, and an impulse to

go up among the house-tops and cry from
them "She is innocent, she is taintlessly
innocent."

XII.

He did not return home, that evening,
until he had sat out the new play at the
Academie, dining beforehand in the restau-
rant of a hotel not far away. The theatre
seldom wearied him, even though the play
was fatally dull. But now, for almost the
only time in his experience, he found it hard
to fix attention upon characters and plot.
Then, during the second act, he felt himself
really *attrapé*. The performance was very
disciplined and intelligent. Besides, he began to recognize the play as something he
had once seen in Paris. Then, a little later,
however, he became confused on this point.
Had he really seen the play, after all? And
at last the truth broke upon him: Belsize had
been pottering and fussing with it. The
"immorality" had been carefully carved
out and something substituted in the result-
ant void. The something struck him as

horribly inharmonious with the original play. It produced an effect of general twist and distortion which made him wonder how the public could deal in such copious plaudits and fail to see that they were bestowed upon material which was altogether the merest harlequinade of life. He now recollected a strong situation in the fourth and final act, and when the curtain had fallen upon the third he wondered what hocus-pocus of "adaptation" Belsize had used with respect to that particular scene. Surely if previous passages had been deemed offensive, this must have proved still more so. But in the French work, however, it had seemed vitally consequential. Even to-night the "way out" looked hardly practicable unless it were used. Would it be used?

The curtain rose on the fourth act, and Fabian soon perceived that it had not been used. And gradually he began to see that a "way out" had been discovered which bore no relation to the real author's treatment. And yet this pulling of lines, this manipulation of events, what were they portending?

16

Suddenly the full truth dawned on Fabian. Belsize had taken from his own play its one most potent and dramatic incident. There it was, boldly, insolently stolen. There could not be the slightest doubt. It was clever enough, as such knavery goes, but it stared at him from behind the footlights with the cool bravado of an unblushing forgery. The text was not his, and yet many drifts both of thought and phrase, wore birth-marks that only guile could have disputed.

The scene "went" with a tremendous *élan*. Its glittering little segment had been slipped adroitly into the general mosaic and shone thence as if the lustre had been borrowed from no unrighteous aid. Fabian felt the shock of disgust which honesty never escapes when it wakes to the fact of its own audacious betrayal. "And this sort of thing," he mused, as he quitted the theatre, "is what meets the conscientious maker of American plays when he seeks decent recognition. Persons like this unscrupulous middleman, Belsize, are those with whom we run the chance of such hideous treacheries."

If his mind had been less weighted by another and sterner trouble he might have sought Belsize at once and taxed him with the cheap, oily fraud so lately compassed. But as it was, he went home. The house was very still and dark when he entered it. He sat for some time brooding in his room before came the desire for rest. And then, as he began to undress, it occurred to him, abruptly and even humorously, that he had been losing all remembrance of Belsize's low deed. A little while ago it would have been so different with him! He would then have thought of bearing his wrong to Eninger and Alicia, and of receiving upon it their discussion, their counsel, their sympathetic indignation.

But during the next few days he found himself ill-at-ease in their company. Alicia had fits of headache which prevented her from always appearing at meals. Eninger was unhabitually tacit and reserved, making his friend wonder at the cause of such moods in him, while feeling confident that he could not have been assailed by any semblance of his own secret worriment.

Little as Fabian realized it, Eninger was tormenting himself with the question: "Can this man possibly merit the suspicion that Gertrude Westerveldt has dared to foster?" His frame of mind was not a jealous one. Its uneasiness came more from a perverse visitation of doubt against which his better sense fought resolutely, as some intellect on the verge of dementia might oppose hallucinations known to be born of bodiless imps and jack-o'-lanterns.

No; he would believe nothing so cruel of one whose honor he had every reason to hold speckless and crystal. More than this: Fabian Dimitry had become an individualism best expressed to him in terms of spirit rather than flesh. Such nobility was a law unto itself, and one no less lovely than cogent. Repeatedly he was on the verge of grasping Fabian's hand and saying to him: "I knew you for years as the perfection of probity; I have known you for a few weeks past as the ideal of generosity; therefore it delights

me to choose you as my chief confidant in
this matter which relates to reckless asper-
sions against yourself."

He did not say these words, or words at
all like them; and yet one evening, after
having been reticent through a dinner from
which Alicia was absent because indisposed,
and during which her father had erected
porcupine-quills with an especial fretfulness,
he paused in the hall beside his friend and
asked him if he would care to smoke for a
little while in the adjacent "office." Thither
they repaired, and seated themselves side by
side. But the mutual constraint was keenly
though indefinitely felt until at last Eninger, with sudden frankness, broke forth:

" Fabian, what do you think *can* ail Alicia?
She's horribly depressed."

" Depressed?" Fabian softly echoed, trying not to look as if this irrelevance had
caused him the least inward start.

" Her trouble defies me," continued Eninger. " It appears to be mental . . and yet I
can't think it serious. You know" (he
turned and looked his companion full in the

eyes) " . . you surely know why any faint
sign of *that* in her should cause me sharpest
dread."

"I know," Fabian replied. Those two
brief little words had a pregnancy and pun-
gency that fifty more could not have aug-
mented.

"The action of her heart is irregular,"
Eninger went on, making a smoke-ring and
then bisecting it with a slant cut of his cigar.
"I'm sure there's no organic malady, however; it's purely functional. If I could once
make up my mind that the root of the diffi-
culty lay there . . but I can't, as yet."

"Why don't you take her away?" asked
Fabian.

"You mean to Europe?"

"Yes. To Switzerland, or better, the Aus-
trian Alps. Somewhere, at least, let us say,
where the air is pure and bracing and she
can have those two mighty means of help,
utter change and utter rest. It might work
marvels."

Eninger made a desperate kind of movement. "Is she really ill enough for that?"

he exclaimed. "Fabian! tell me just how ill you think she is! I confess that I've failed to find out. Perhaps your layman's eyes are keener than my professional ones."

Eninger had now risen from his chair; he stood beside that of Fabian, with one hand resting on the shoulder of his friend.

"I have noticed a change," came the awaited answer, though it was not at all swift in coming. "But this change has not struck me as a marked one. A little delay ought to work no harm."

"You mean," queried Eninger, "a watching for new symptoms?"

"Yes."

"And as to calling in another physician?"

"If I had the least doubt I would do so."

"And yet you counsel delay."

"Ah," said Fabian, with depths of earnestness in his liquid and shining look, "do not, my friend, misunderstand me. There are genuine fears of danger and there are false ones. Try to discover the true foundation of yours—whether it be rock or sand."

"It is so hard," muttered Eninger, "to judge fairly where we love fondly."

"Or where we hate foolishly," said Fabian, as if to himself, and no doubt thinking of Mrs. Atterbury.

"How is that?" asked Eninger, with a little start. And then his thoughts drifted to Gertrude Westerveldt. "Right, indeed," he added, in another moment.

The anxiety felt for Alicia by her husband became to Fabian a source of increasing torment during the next few hours. His love had been held in leash by duty, fortitude, moral strength, until now. But now it broke bonds and flooded his soul with misery. She was ill and he could not be close beside her, to comfort her. Eninger, whom she loved—whom he was certain that she loved—stood near her, of course. It was not, to his high soul, a question of whom she preferred; it was a burning and piercing question as to the capacity of this or that human soul who could help her the more. All sorts of ways in which men and women love have been dissected and examined; this age we live in teems with such disclosures. But

there is a self-abnegating way, a way as
divine as earthly intelligence can conceive
of what is divine, which analysis, vivisec-
tion, realism has not yet presumed to touch.
These methods recoil from such expression,
afraid of it as an untruth, a mere midsum-
mer madness jarring our mortal brain and
nerves. But many a modern annalist recoils
before a passion which through meagre
knowledge of life he conceives impossible.
That kind of a passion was Fabian Dimitry's.

He saw how self-annihilatingly he loved
Alicia. His past course had seemed to make
this plain; his present summons (as if from
heights on heights of infinite command and
exhortation) made it plainer still. He was
without all religious faith; like thousands
of other nineteenth-century thinkers, he was
deist, pantheist, agnostic, atheist, all blended
into one. From a certain point of view he
did not know what he believed; from another
point of view he knew too fatally well how
much, how apprehensively much, he disbe-
lieved. But the meaning of social mo-
rality was clear to him. He had shown it in

renouncing Alicia. The pulses of his heart—
every sturdy stroke—beat still toward an
attainment of this one single goal: to repress
carnal ardor and stay the unflinching sentinel
of his own down-trodden desires. We never
conquer an earthly longing, we humans, but
something rises from it, spiritual in significance as the odor that floods air when some
brute hoof smites a bed of violets. Fabian
had, if you please, this recompense of sacrifice. He did not call it spiritual; he called
it by no name except one which the ghost-
worshipers and pietists of the world would
have sneered at as material. Chastity and
sublimity of love engendered it, and this
truth he recognized, realized. But he was
capable of facing what so few emotional
spirits have ever had the mental equipoise
to confront: the loftier lore of existence
needs no ritual or hymnal for its confirma-
tion, being rooted in the evolution of dust
toward divinity, of grossness toward great-
ness. He did not seek a supernatural reason
why he would be willing to die for the woman
he loved. The natural reason, shorn of fancy-

bred sentiment, sufficed him. He loved just as
purely and deeply while admitting the ancestry of the ape. He plunged into no shadowy
conduits of tradition to verify his present
fealty. It was there, and it had sprung from
the monstrous push and sweep of things, like
the delicate skeleton of a forest-leaf, like the
huge anatomy of the mastodon. His passion
had the actuality of the green in grass, the
authenticity of the redness in roses, the
beauty of the pomp in dawns, the power of
the horror in lightning. He accepted it,
wishing but not seeking to explain its origin. He had conquered much in the terri-
tory of his love; self-command had swept
away this thicket, had forded that river.
But an uninvaded tract remained. It defied
him. Residual, it was also inviolate. Was
it not holy, was it not clad with a soft, yet
splendid sanctity as well? Still worshiping
the woman he had loved first, last and absolutely, he longed to guard her, aid her, save
her, give mind, blood, bone, thew, nerve
sacrificially in her behalf.

The next day, as it chanced, was the one

which fate and society had conspired to sanctify as that of the Verrinder-Van Wagenen wedding. Fabian breakfasted late, and consequently alone. He soon discovered that Eninger had several patients who sought consultation with him in his office and that Alicia was closeted upstairs. Fabian's night had been almost a sleepless one, but he now breasted a raw, rainy day and went "down town" to meet certain financial calls there. Returning at about four o'clock in the afternoon, disconcerted and a little unstrung by the sordidness and clamor of Wall Street, he chanced to meet Alicia in the lower hall. She was gayly and prettily dressed, as if for some afternoon festivity. She had a slightly tired look about the eyes, but her face betrayed no signs of ill-health.

"Have you forgotten your engagement?" she asked, giving him her hand.

"You've the advantage of me, I confess," he returned, coloring a little.

"Don't you remember that we were to go to Miss Van Wagenen's wedding in one another's company?"

"Is it really to-day? I'd quite forgotten about it."

But he had only a few changes of toilet to make, and Alicia promptly agreed that she would wait for him. The distance they had to walk was but one or two streets. It had grown less inclement, and a powdery snow-fall had given place to flying purplish clouds and winds that seemed to battle with one another like contending spirits. "I'm glad you feel strong enough to go," Fabian said, as they walked along with heads bowed a little before the hardihood of the blasts.

"Thanks," she replied. "I'm better this afternoon. I feel really quite strong."

"Then you were weak yesterday?"

"Horridly. I had moments when it seemed as if I could scarcely move. I didn't tell Ray. That is, when he asked me how I felt, I didn't tell him just how forlorn my sensations were."

"Was that right?" returned Fabian. "Should you not have told him? Remember, he is your physician besides being . . ."

"My husband?" she supplied, as he paused.

"Oh, of course. But I . . well, I meant, just then, that he is more."

"More?"

"The man you've grown to love above all others."

She was silent for a moment. And then she broke out, gently but with fervor:

"Don't say 'grown to love' above all others. He's my first and only love. All else now seems phantom-like. I thought we had a full talk on that subject, and that you understood."

He did not immediately answer. But after a slight while he said: "Yes; you are right. I should have remembered. Pardon me. Not that I've ever forgotten that talk—in which you told me of your consent to have me come and live under the same roof with you . . "

"And with Ray," she amended, composedly.

"And with Ray," he conceded. "Not, indeed, that I ever can forget it, though I should live a thousand years."

"Do you mean that it was . . painful?"

"Painful?" he repeated. . . And then he said no more, since they had reached the portals of the spacious Van Wagenen residence, where footmen were sentinelled both outside and beneath a striped awning and carriages waited in smart, glossy cohorts.

The drawing-rooms were jammed, and all the town was there. Young Mrs. Verrinder looked radiant and riant in her pearls and point-lace, beside the Honorable Cecil, her newly-created husband. For a time Alicia and Fabian became separated. Then, near one of the doorways, they met again, and he said to her carelessly:

"You're not going just yet, are you?"

"No," she replied. "Mr. Van Nostrand asked me to go upstairs and look at the presents. But an old lady begged him to get her an ice, and we've been torn asunder in consequence."

"Won't you come up with me, then?" said Fabian; and soon they were ascending the staircase together.

It was a sumptuous array of bridal gifts.

The room in which it had been spread forth was densely thronged. Pressing and jostling were inevitable. Alicia was unusually quiet as her gaze fell on the various costly and charming objects. Fabian kept as near to her as possible, though sometimes they were parted. During an incident of the latter sort and while three or four people had managed to elbow and wedge their forms between Alicia and himself, a sudden harsh and poignant thought entered Fabian's head.

It made him bite his lip and use little ceremony in rejoining her. And then he observed that she had grown very pale. "It may be the heat of the rooms," he thought. "I won't ask her if she is ill; that might only cause her to feel worse."

Aloud he said to her: "Had we not better quit this close room?"

"Do you find it unpleasant?" she asked.

"Yes. Do you?"

"A little. . ." She turned to a man who had just slipped up to her side and spoken several low words. He had a smooth face and a gentlemanlike air. You could not have told him from the guests, but he was not a guest. He had been posted here to guard all this opulence, and he did not always mingle, by any means, with the rich and sleek. He was a fish that often swam in other waters than those of elegance and caste.

"I know nothing of the matter," Fabian heard Alicia say, as if with annoyance, to this person. "Did I not tell you so before?"

"Of what matter?" came Fabian's involuntary question. Just then he perceived Mrs. Westerveldt and Mrs. Atterbury standing together near by, as though in amical converse—an event fit to shake to their roots the especial cliques of which either lady was a member. They had ceased to talk, and were watching Mrs. Eninger and the man who had just inaudibly conferred with her. Mrs. Atterbury was also watching Fabian, whose face betrayed not a little anxiety. In response to his inquiry Alicia said, with a trembling voice and oddly excited manner:

"Never mind. Come down-stairs. Please come directly."

17

Fabian felt rooted to the floor. She forced her way out of the room. The man who had spoken to her did not follow her, but his eyes met Fabian's with a look of mingled perplexity and disgust.

At least so Fabian read the look. In another instant he saw that Mrs. Atterbury was beckoning to him. He made an effort and joined her, bowing to Mrs. Westerveldt and herself with one inclusive salute. If he had been less perturbed he would have wondered at her daring to signal to him like this after their recent stormy parting.

The man who had addressed Alicia now followed him.

"Excuse me, sir," this person said, "but will you please tell me the name of the lady you just spoke with?"

Fabian did not reply. A few seconds passed, and then with her hardest and clearest tones Mrs. Westerveldt volunteered to say:

"The lady's name is Mrs. Eninger."

"Eninger," repeated the man. "Thank you." And he glided away.

It seemed to Fabian as if the heart in his breast had turned to a lump of ice.

XIII.

This meeting of Gertrude Westerveldt and
Adela Atterbury, the two arch-foes, had just
now a unique force of significance. It was
one of a series that continued from year to
year; these two ladies, each furtively detesting and disapproving the other, always made
a point of exchanging verbal courtesies once
a season. The rest of the time it was a
punctilious exchange of pasteboard and an
arctic-antarctic avoidance.

Fabian looked Mrs. Westerveldt full in
the eyes after she had spoken Alicia's name.
"Do you know who that gentleman is?" he
inquired. He was still uncertain regarding
the custodian of the Van Wagenen golconda,
and so used "gentleman" as the word in
best probable taste.

"Yes," said Mrs. Westerveldt, whom he
had merely bowed to for years and had
always gauged as frigid and small in spirit,

with perhaps that intuition born of a spirit warm and spacious. "Yes, Mr. Dimitry, I do know him. I happened to learn just now, while I was glancing over the presents. *You* told me, didn't you?" and she looked across her shoulder at one of her inseparable male allies, a man with a huge nosegay of gardenias in the lapel of his frock-coat.

·The adherent smiled and nodded. "You mean the detective," he said. "I'm *almost* sure he's one. Anyway, Jack Laight assured me he was, and Jack is a great collector of gossip."

Mrs. Westerveldt seemed to absorb herself in watching Fabian. "I've just been speaking to your friend, Mrs. Atterbury," she said, "on the subject of your friend, Mrs. Eninger."

"Ah," returned Fabian, feeling that his cheeks must be like paper. "And did you hear" (he met Adela Atterbury's eyes, now) "what savage things one excellent woman is sometimes capable of saying about another?"

"By no means," began Mrs. Westerveldt,

with her neatest suavity. "The truth is, we . . "

But Fabian heard no more. People broke past him, going toward the rich-laden board, and he felt pierced by the sudden sense that to stay longer in this crowded room might make him say or do some mad thing. His ears rang, his brain spun, as he gained the head of the staircase.

Where was Alicia? Reaching the lower hall, he stood still for a moment, eager to find her, yet hopeless what method of search to adopt. Then, suddenly but very quietly, a hand touched his shoulder. He recognized a smooth-shaven, decorous face; he had so lately seen it upstairs.

"Mrs. Eninger has left the house if you are looking for her," said the same voice which he had heard so short a while ago.

Hardly knowing what he answered, Fabian returned: "You are sure? You followed her down-stairs?"

The babble here in this hall was so great, and the music played so voluminously, near at hand, that mighty state-secrets could have been talked of between these two men without even a dim chance of anyone over-hearing.

"Yes," replied the man. "I saw that lady leave the house. And I've just whispered a word about her to Mrs. Van Wagenen."

"Yes? What did you say?"

"I told the lady of the house what I suspected."

"Suspected?" shot back Fabian, catching at the word.

"Yes, sir."

"Well . . what did you suspect?"

The man lowered his eyelids for an instant. That "sir" had told Fabian his place and capacity in a trice.

"I have my duty to do," came the reply. "I'm needed upstairs now; I can't wait."

"Very well. Go on."

"I . . thought the lady's dress might have caught in it, and that it was swept off the table. I asked her, but she gave me only a queer, half-angry kind of answer."

"'It,' you say? What was 'it'?"

"A small, silver paper-cutter, with some initials in diamonds. Small, as I say, but very valuable."

Fabian drew a long, deep breath. "What did you *see?*" he queried, with one ransacking glance of desperation that swept the man's placid face and then dropped away from it.

Again the eyelids were lowered for a second, and then lifted. "I *saw* nothing. But the lady took up the paper-cutter—that I *did* see. Then something turned my attention elsewhere, and when I looked again it was gone. It had a filigreed handle—little gold flowers that stuck out from the solid part with stems and leaves, you understand. That's why I thought it might have got fastened to her frock or sleeves, or something like that."

Fabian tried to smile as if in contemptuous disbelief. "It may be on the floor now," he said.

"No, sir. I searched; I searched like a ferret."

"How long did your search take?"

"Oh, I've got sharp eyes," said the man, with a bluff ring of annoyance in his voice— one that sounded as though he would never bend his full-bloomed Americanism again to the utterance of another "sir."

"And you found nothing?" came Fabian's next words.

"No—nothing."

"And you *think* . . ?" But Fabian paused, there. "Excuse me," he broke off; "you've seen Mrs. Van Wagenen?"

"Yes."

"And told her—what?"

"What I suspect."

"You gave her a . . a certain name?"

"I gave her Mrs. Eninger's name."

"Ah," exclaimed Fabian, with a low voice and yet with one that seemed to himself as if it rang from his heart's bleeding core, "tell me what proof—what real proof, did you give Mrs. Van Wagenen in return for your fancies—your silly, insolent, black-guardly fancies?" He was taller than his companion, and for an instant glared down upon him with scathing rebuke.

His anger roused anger in the man he addressed. "Proof!" came the retort, "I've told Mrs. Van Wagenen what I think. *I* don't care. I'm only here to see what you big folks do. You were close at her side. Perhaps *you* took it. *I* couldn't swear. You may have. I didn't ask *your* name. I'm new in this kind o' business. I've seen fellows fine-looking as you, that were . . "

Fabian's ire was quite lulled. He broke away from the speaker. Luckily there was a little side-room, down here in this main hall, where he had left coat and hat. He procured both as quickly as he could. All the while he felt as if a hand were clutching his arm, a voice were hissing in his ear.

He got out into the spring twilight. The strip of heaven above the housetops was dim and yet cloudless; it seemed to wait for the first cold, silver advent of the stars—"The stars," flashed through his mind in a vagrancy of musing, "that shine with equal scorn over town and prairie, telling us nothing . . nothing!"

Half way in the direction of his home, he

paused. Was that man following him? No
. . he squared himself and looked to the
right, the left, and searchingly down the
line of street he had just pursued.

"*You were close at her side. Perhaps you
look it.*"

The man had said that. Those words kept
ringing in his ears. He walked onward, and
found himself brooding in a strange, new
way.

"*Perhaps you took it.*"

He could not escape those few piercing
words. They haunted him as he ascended
the stoop of his home and let himself in with
his latch-key.

A servant chanced to be in the rear part
of the hall. "Has Mrs. Eninger returned?"
he asked.

"Yes, sir," came the answer; "she got
back a few minutes ago."

"Is she upstairs?"

"Yes, sir."

"Say that I would like to see her here—
in the drawing-room, at once. Stay, please."

"Well, sir?"

" Is Mr. Eninger at home?"

" No, sir."

" All right.   Carry my order."

Fabian went into the pretty drawing-room, full of etchings and tapestries that he had helped to dispose.   That task had been so pleasant during recent days.   Great changes had been wrought here since he had come to live with them.   They used to laugh at him and call him "the æsthete."   Alicia would slip in, with her smile, her voice, her white, graceful, restless hands. . .   And now! . . He bowed his head.   He had no tears to weep—or so it seemed to him—unless they were drops of blood.

Presently the servant came back and said that Mrs. Eninger was not very well and would see him upstairs in her dressing-room.

" Very well," he replied, " I will go up."

He felt much stronger and firmer as he crossed the threshold of the room where Alicia sat.   He shut the door behind him.

" *You were close at her side.   Perhaps you took it.*"

How those words kept knelling themselves through his brain!

Alicia was seated in an arm-chair, with her bonnet off and her street-mantle unbuttoned.

Fabian took a seat at her side. "You came straight home," he said, watching her in her pallor and forlornness.

"Yes, I came straight home."

"They know what you did there," he continued. "They are talking of it. You have been found out."

She rose from the chair and clasped both hands together. Then she suddenly sank at Fabian's feet.

"Oh, my God!" she murmured. "What will become of me?"

He stooped and raised her quivering form. "There, sit down again," he said, "and tell me everything."

"Everything?" she gasped, looking at him with the dazed stare of a child who has been caught in some odious act.

"Yes. You know what I mean. Begin at the beginning and don't omit a detail. Won't you consent to this?"

She did not at once reply, but soon her voice faltered "yes." She had clasped her hands again; her head was bent, and as she continued to speak he observed that it swayed slightly from side to side. The voice that she used was her own inalienably lovely one. How sad to hear its familiar music enfold the confession that now came from her!

"I first had the desire in London, a year or two before we were married. It came upon me at a shop in Bond Street; the things were all of ivory and very nice; it was near Christmas. I was horrified at myself and spent several hours in tears, thinking over my narrow escape. For the impulse had been almost ungovernable. If another returned to me, what should I do hereafter? It was not that I did not loathe the thought of being a thief, or that I craved the mere possession of things which did not belong to me. It was wholly different from all that. . . I can't explain it; I've tortured myself trying to explain it, but I've never succeeded. I've prayed, for hours at a time, to be delivered from the temptation, the curse, the malady. With tears streaming down my cheeks I've prayed! But God has never

heard me. I wanted to tell Ray after I first
lost control. It was not till I'd married him
and come here. It was one evening at a
supper given after a theatre-party by Mrs.
Gansevoort. You recall it, don't you? You
were there. I was left alone for a few minutes
near a little table loaded with pretty things.
I . . I took—you said you wanted me not
to omit a detail," she broke off, and lifted
to him the humid blue of her glittering
eyes.

"Not one—not one," he answered.

Then she went on. He heard it all. It
was sickening, yet it tore his heart with pity
for her.

At last he said, while she sat before him
choked and shuddering:

"You've told everything, have you not?
There's nothing more?"

"Nothing," she sobbed. Her confession
had terribly racked her. His vast compassion made him almost reel as he now rose.
He had the yearning to seize her in his arms
and comfort her for the anguish that he was
certain she felt—the anguish born of a hor-

rible conscious madness, inflicted on her by
the fierce hand of heredity, reaching from
her dead ancestors' graves.

But he spoke very quietly while standing
beside her. "Will you get me everything
you have taken—*everything*, mind! Will
you put all into a package and leave them
in my room as soon as you can! Will you
do this! Do you understand me perfectly?"

"Yes," she said, looking up at him again
in her despair.

He knotted his hands, that he might keep
from rushing toward her and putting them
about her neck. He had loved her so profoundly—he loved her so profoundly still!
Had she not once been his idol, his sweetheart, his delight! And from then till now
had his love ever lessened or faded! Was it
not because of this very madness in her
(possible then, tangible and fearful now!)
that he had renounced her, given her up for
another to woo and win?

Again he spoke with calmness. "You
must try and compose yourself. It still
wants nearly an hour of dinner-time. When

Ray returns I hope you will meet him without agitation. And remember about the
package. I will do all I can for you. Everything may not be lost yet. You have been
ill—very ill, and neither Ray nor I suspected.
But there is still hope."

"Hope?" she murmured.

"Yes. Things might be worse for you
than they are. And in a little while you
will be cared for as you should have been
cared for if we had only guessed sooner."

Still once more she swept his face with her
dolorous eyes. "Oh, God bless you!" she said.
"You call it an illness, but many people will
not allow that it is. I shall be steeped in
disgrace, even if I'm not dragged to prison.
And Ray—poor Ray! It will be so horrible
for him! But then you say everything may
not be lost yet! What do you mean by that?
What do you mean by saying there is still
hope, and that things might be worse for me
than they are?"

He went closer to her and let his hand fall
on her arm. "I mean to do my very best,
Alicia," he said. She started a little at hear-

18

ing him pronounce her name; she had not
heard it from his lips since the old days
when they were betrothed lovers. He caught
one of her hands and pressed it to his lips
passionately, twice, thrice. Then a flush
mantled his face, as though of sharp shame.
He turned away and hurried toward the
door. "Remember your promise," he said,
just before passing from the room.

She did not see the great melancholy in
his look as these words left him.

He soon went out of doors into the windy
spring twilight, and presently a cab was
taking him to the house of Mrs. Atterbury.

She had just dismissed her carriage and
was entering her own doorway, when he
alighted from his vehicle. By a glance
across her shoulder she recognized him.

"I thought you would probably come,"
she said, low of voice, as they stood in the
hall together. And then she added: "Even
though you did leave me in so savage a mood
when we last met."

He made no reply, but followed her into
the reception-room just off the hall, where

two or three lamps had been lighted, big, rich-hued stars in the partial dusk.

They seated themselves. She loosened her bonnet-strings and tossed her bonnet on a near chair. Just as she did so he began to speak.

"Call my mood savage, if you please. Yours had surely been . . accusative. But I came to ask you——"

"About *her*," struck in his hearer, not harshly, yet in a way that lacked all native warmth. "I was prepared for that." And then, with a suddenly hardening face, she proceeded in the manner that he had often known her to employ when most earnest—the manner that some people termed rowdy, as it has been recorded: "On my word of honor I'm sorry I told you that you lied to save her. But good heavens, hasn't to-day proved it?"

"Proved it?" he said, pale to the lips, as she looked at him. "Did the Van Wagenen policeman prove it? No; he did not. He told me, in so many words, that he could not."

Mrs. Atterbury's eyes flashed. "He didn't search her, if you mean that, you . . you madman!"

He laughed, and at once exclaimed: "Madman! Oh, yes, you're no doubt right. I dare say I *am* a madman."

"Why, what else can you be," came her swift, defiant answer, "when you presume to tell me that she didn't show this evening every sign of guilt? He went to Mrs. Van Wagenen, that man; he let her know just what had happened. I saw her afterward; so did Mrs. Westerveldt. She was furious. You'll hear from her to-morrow, I suppose. Not *you*, of course, but your people—your family—the household you've been wise and sane enough to make yourself a part of. Look here, now, Fabian Dimitry, I don't mean one grain of malice. But *oh*, how you've been fooled by that woman! Gertrude Westerveldt is sick with disgust at her. It was funny—it almost made me laugh right out, serious as I felt—to think of Gertrude and me ever putting our heads together and actually agreeing on any one earthly sub-

ject. But gracious goodness, man, I found
Gertrude had missed a turquoise ring off her
dressing-table one night when your paragon
had dined at her house and had afterward
stood close to the very spot where the ring
was laid. But bless you, this wasn't all.
Gertrude dropped on the floor, at another
time, a little spray of diamonds when she
was upstairs with my lady Eninger after a
dinner at her own home in Forty-Second
Street. And this cousin of mine (whom I
don't like, as I'm sure you know, but whom
I've never caught in a falsehood as long as
we've gone on mutually hating one another)
declares that she had reason to feel almost
certain her jewel was impudently pocketed
there before her very eyes."

"Reason to feel *almost* certain!" said
Fabian. "The 'almost' has been discreetly
used by Mrs. Westerveldt. It is the same,
no doubt, as *your* 'almost certain,' on
another occasion, when you opened that cabinet of curios."

"Ah," cried Mrs. Atterbury, springing to
her feet, "this is preposterous!"

"I think it so, too," returned Fabian, slowly rising.

She spoke in a half-strangled voice. "Do you mean *still* to claim that the woman's innocent? Do you mean to stick up for her innocence *now*, when we three (Mrs. Van Wagenen, Gertrude and I) are all prepared to bring charges against her?"

He inclined his head as if in sarcastic assent. "So you've decided to do that?"

"Yes—we have! The whole thing is a glaring outrage, and should be suppressed, punished."

"You've taken your course, then?"

"Mrs. Van Wagenen has. You'll hear from her quite soon, and she has been given full authority to use our names."

"I see," said Fabian; "it's gone that far."

"Yes," retorted the little lady, trembling with wrath. "It *has* gone that far, and we mean it shall go further."

"Ah, you mean this, do you?" . . Something in his intonation made her look at him with surprise breaking through her anger.

"Have you considered certain points of this case?" he went on, with a voice bell-like, vibrant, and yet oddly opposite to his wonted tones. "Have you recollected that Mrs. Westerveldt discharged her maid for stealing the turquoise ring you have mentioned? I chance to know that this is true, for the maid brought suit against her former mistress, and I saw a notice of the expected legal proceedings in a newspaper of eight or ten days ago. Now the maid may be guilty or the reverse: that remains to be shown. But Mrs. Westerveldt, in accusing her, has made it plain that she thinks the maid guilty. 'Oh, very well,' you may say, 'but there were other things taken besides the turquoise ring, and there were other times of alleged theft on the part of her we think the thief.' Very good. Count over those times; consider them. You'll find they all have one point in common."

"One point in common. I don't understand. Do you mean that they were all brazen acts?"

"I mean this: that whenever you suspected

Alicia Eninger *I was somewhere near her.* . . .
Ah, now I perceive that you *do* understand."

He walked toward the hall in another minute, and looked at her across his shoulder. He gave her, as it were, a smile of farewell; but the smile teemed with a terrible mockery and despair.

"It *can't* be true," she broke out, "that you're willing— No! no!" And she hurried after him through the *portière* whose folds were still agitated from his exit.

But he had already caught up his hat from a table in the hall, and now he seized the knob of the front door.

"Fabian!" she exclaimed, at this point.

"Well?" he returned, pausing and looking at her.

"Will you throw your honor to the dogs just to save that worthless creature?"

"She is innocent," he said, his voice not raised in the least, yet his mien simply imperial through its challenging denial. "These charges have been brought against the wrong person."

"And the right one is . . ?"

"Myself."

He at once opened the door and disappeared. Mrs. Atterbury went back into the reception-room and for some little time she sat quite still, except that now and then she visibly shuddered.

If he had sworn to her a hundred times what he had just stated, and sworn it each time with some new and very sacred oath, she would not have believed him. Of course it was untrue. And the madness of him, to take that awful burden on his shoulders! Had not this wily woman already cost him enough pain! That she should drag him now into self-ruin was monstrous, incredible.

The tears stole to Adela Atterbury's eyes, and by and by her sobs followed. She sat there and wept in the soft lustre of the lamps. At the same time a cold fear was slipping about her heart, like some chill tide that creeps round a stranded shell.

Whatever Fabian Dimitry had resolved on he would carry out. She knew him well enough to be certain that if he had clearly determined to damn himself in the eyes of the world he would take care that this damnation should be accomplished after no bungling fashion.

Her hardy nature for once recoiled before the threatened purpose of another, and recoiled in a paralysis of dismay. What expedient of preventive could she light on? Would to-morrow bring any? No; for the man's insensate devotion would prove not less strong than the passion that inspired it.

"If Lewsy should come in and find me here like this," she thought, "and if I should tell him who's forced these tears from me, wouldn't he for once in our married life be downright jealous?"

Oddly enough, and yet as many a woman will do under like mental siege, she let this wholly foreign idea of "Lewsy" drift through her preoccupied brain.

But she was doubtless quite wrong. Lewsy would not have dreamed of being jealous. He would probably have confided to some Wall Street friend, as they lunched at the Beaver Street Delmonico's next day, that

"My wife, by Jove, has got one of the biggest and most sympathetic hearts in America!"

He would have vaunted her heart, poor Lewsy, as he vaunted everything she possessed, from the trim of her wit to the cut of her finger-nail. Happy the husband who believes that he holds the lounging-room in that mystic domicile, his wife's affection, and who has not yet convinced himself that this haunt of ease is but a deftly-upholstered ante-chamber!

XIV.

"I thought you were Ray," said the Colonel to Fabian, as the latter passed toward his own room along an upper hall. "Bless me, what *is* keeping dinner from being served?"

"Are you hungry?" said Fabian, passing the speaker and scarcely knowing what reply he gave.

"Am I hungry!" gruffly exploded the Colonel. "What an American sort of answer!" He stood with eye-glasses poised in one hand, gazing after the friend of his son-in-law.

"But it only confirms my already fixed creed—for the people of this queer land dinner has no sanctity, none whatever! They do not dine; they feed—often with haphazard haste and seldom with either punctuality or dignity."

Fabian failed to hear these last withering words. He entered his own room, and at

once his eye lit on an expected package.
Locking himself against intrusion, he opened
it. The contents, having been eagerly surveyed, stung and racked him. Alicia had
kept her word. The turquoise ring was
here, and this he trod into an almost shape-
less mass as soon as he had found it. Then
he opened the window and flung down into
the street the tiny golden wreck thus wrought.
Scarcely had he done so, when Eninger
knocked at his door. "Fabian," soon came
the anxious question, "can you tell me what
has made Alicia so forlorn?" As he spoke
thus, Eninger crossed the threshold, with
head somewhat bowed and hands locked
behind him. "I returned home a little
while ago," he went on, "and was amazed at
meeting her. She is very feeble in strength,
and hysterical in behavior. Has anything
occurred this afternoon at the Van Wagen-
ens' which could possibly have unnerved her
like this?"

Fabian seemed lost in thought. Then his
reverie gave place to a sudden ardor. "Oh,
my poor Ray," he said, "a great deal has

happened that you know nothing of—
nothing! Would to heaven I could shirk
the telling of it! . . There, sit down—pray
sit down and hear me. I must say certain
things. You've never dreamed of what I
must explain to you. Ray, believe me, it
will hit you hard. It will be all the worse to
a sensitive and fastidious fellow like you.
Ray! you *will* prove a man, won't you,
while I tell it!"

He had pushed Eninger into a chair, and
now stood over him with a hand on each of
his shoulders. Eninger, grown very pale,
simply nodded and said:

" Well. . . It concerns *her*, of course."

"Yes." . . And then, for what may have
been ten full minutes, Fabian spoke. Once
or twice the auditor closed his eyes and
palpably trembled. At these times Fabian
would seize his hand, briefly but forcibly
pressing it.

Then, at last, there was dead silence.
Fabian waited to be answered. Eninger
looked like a man to whom the utterance of
even one word would be crucial. Still, he
presently replied:

"How ghastly it all sounds! . . Ah, my friend, you are avenged for the way I behaved to you in London!"

"Hush, Ray. It *is* ghastly, but there's this about it—you can pardon her."

"Pardon her?"

"The curse of an inherited madness! Why not? It has been kleptomania; it might have been one of a hundred cerebral ills. And Ray, consider this: you know, now, what it is, and can fight it."

"Fight it?"

"To the death. Take her away for a year at least. Watch her with one absorbing aim. Set yourself a task in the crystal air of some quiet mountain retreat, and vow that love shall tear victory from science. Send the Colonel back to England; do not permit yourself a single emotion that does not relate to her cure. In the end you will conquer; she will be restored to you, her sane and lovely self."

"Restored to me!" Eninger broke out, in bitterness. "And how? Disgraced before the world—branded by a stigma ineffaceable!"

"Not so, Ray. I . . I have thought of a certain method by which all that may be avoided."

"What can you mean? Avoided? Why, haven't you already told me that this horror is being babbled about?"

"Suspicions have sprung up; they can be refuted. I've a plan, Ray, and I want to act it out. To-night I shall be busy thinking it over. To-morrow you and I will talk of it, definitely, in detail. Meanwhile, do all that you can for *her;* watch her with your best professional caution; but don't show her the faintest sign, as yet, that you've heard these unhappy truths about her."

"Your plan is but a dream, I'm sure," said Eninger, whose face already looked ravaged by agony. "I thank you for the great-heartedness that has prompted you to imagine it, but——"

"No, Ray; imagination is not all of it, I promise you! Trust me till to-morrow!" . .

But Eninger's thoughts were of Gertrude Westerveldt and the scornful hints he had

heard from her in their last interview. He
read the real meaning of those hints now,
but in this new guise they made him discern
how implacable a cruelty that woman might
be prepared to reveal.

"Trust me till to-morrow," nevertheless
rang comfortingly in his ears as he passed
from Fabian's room to rejoin his wife. Ah,
why should he not strive to trust so peerless a
friend as this man had already proved himself! Where was there such wisdom blended
with such benignancy! Did he ever counsel
at random, and was there not a constant
sweet premeditation in all his deeds, as
though even a spirit so capable of sacrifice
knew how to temper its generosity with a
telling leaven of prudence!

Fabian, left alone, went to his writing-desk
and seated himself before it. A servant soon
came to tell him that dinner waited, but he
shrank from food as though in this case it
meant to sit at meat with the Borgias.
Neither Mr. nor Mrs. Eninger, the servant
told him, had yet appeared in the dining-
room; but the Colonel had appeared there
and had begun to dine.

19

A grim picture of this personage thrust itself into Fabian's fancy. "How savage and gaunt the old fellow must look," it floated through his mind, "seated down there sipping his soup in 'ancient, solitary reign'! If one really had the heart to break bread with him, what an uncanny fellow-feaster would he seem."

For a good while after the servant had gone from him, Fabian sat musing over certain letters which he desired to write. Addressed to several different persons, these letters must all be in the form of guilty confessions and be also the premonitions of a determined flight. They would not be sent until he had made arrangements of another and a financial sort. Ray should receive a certain share of his property: the rest he would take with him into Brazil. His departure would shine balefully as an admission of personal shame. Each article stolen by Alicia he would return to its rightful possessor, with the statement that he had been the thief of it, not she. At first he might not be credited. But afterward . .

Somehow his broodings, while he sat and gave them sway, had caught the trick of pausing just there.

Would people, even eventually, believe him? Would they not say . . ?—Ah, how this "plan" to which he had lately referred with such confidence in the hearing of Eninger, now became engirt with chances of failure! He had not seen them until to-night, when they slipped their cold little pleas and protests into his consciousness. That resolved flight of his might accomplish nothing for *her*. It might be named the mere flimsy scheme of a love-sick worshiper.

But . . was there any *other* way?

He rose, pushing aside some sheets of notepaper on whose blankness he had not yet left a single line. The desire beset him to think while walking in the open air. He passed down-stairs, finding the two halls which he traversed quite vacant and still.

Once out in the street, he discovered that all harsh weather-signs had fled and that the town was canopied by one of those mild yet limpid nights which bring the infinite

nearer to man   He walked slowly along,
letting his eyes again and again roam the
star-studded slopes of heaven.   Creation,
how monstrous it was!—we, its products yet
its puny minions, how piteously we compared
with it!   And yet the whole terrible scheme
of the universe might be, and doubtless was,
a mere sightless, mute, self-moving force.
It had created Jupiter and Canopus—one of
a million giant planets, one of a million
giant suns.   But from its mystic funds had
also sprung a power, an efflorescence, grander
though subtler than these.   Love had been
born thence—human love, with all its base
leases and costs, with all its high restraints
and rewards.   Did not he who loves unself-
ishly fling in the teeth of death a divine
challenge!   No matter if he perished eter-
nally when the last breath left his lips.   In
the future making of men his example
should find its inevitable place.   Like the
breaking of a huge wave far out at sea, it
would shape ripples that must mingle with
the tides of distant coasts.

To sacrifice one's self wholly for a pure

love! Was it so hard, after all, that the world should laud it as so lofty! . . This flying in hypocritic cowardice of guilt to Brazil, to Heaven knew where . . how could such course actually end but with the entail of sluggish, dragging misery! And then the possible meagreness of the proffered help! How that result would degrade, belittle, minimize the whole deed! Dying to save one we love were an act that might set the bounds for its own dignity. Merely lying from the same motive would be to build defences round loopholes tempting the ingress of ridicule!

. . . When Fabian went back to his home, that night, the hour was a little past eleven, and the house no less dark than quiet. He went down to the door of Eninger's office on the basement-floor. Vacancy and gloom here: he had expected—feared, indeed—to find his friend seated in this familiar room. With the aid of his own match-box he lit a jet of gas. The rays appeared to focus themselves on a uniform row of phials that filled one special shelf. Only such a little time

ago he and Eninger had had a certain toxo-
logic talk, and then . . . But no matter;
there was what he wished; its dark little
labelled cube gleamed as harmless as if
brimming with juices brewed from violets.
. . . He presently turned off the gas and
went upstairs. In the dimness, while pausing at a particular door, he heard the sound
of voices. Hating to listen, he nevertheless
did so now. " For this once in my life," he
said to himself, sworn foe as he had always
been of every act which the least taint of
meanness could soil.

"I have not once dreamed of blaming
you," he heard Eninger say. " I blame
only myself, for not having surmised how
ill you really were. . . You speak of Fabian; he has some strange conviction that he
can arrest the scandal. Had anyone but
himself told me of such a purpose I would
simply have felt its entire hopelessness.
But he, so trustworthy and so capable . .
perhaps he may have found a way, after
all."

Fabian moved toward his own room. " You

are right," he said to himself, in a soft whisper; " I *have* found a way."

For several hours he wrote letters. Each was a confession of personal guilt and yet a declaration as well that an unconquerable insanity had caused him to behave as he had done. He mentioned the suspicions formed against Alicia as hideous injustice, and stated that more than once he had tried to make it seem as if she were the real culprit.

These letters were terribly ingenious, and to each he attached a small packet containing one or more of the stolen objects. Every letter, too, contained the assertion that when its pages were read by the eyes for which they were intended he should have ceased to live.

All was now performed except one final task—his letter to Ray Eninger. This he took a long time to write, and filled with the burning eloquence of entreaty. He implored Eninger to let the true reason of his deed remain forever wrapped in secrecy. He assured him that no reluctance went with it —that it seemed to him then, at that mid-

night hour, like a beautiful and luminous
pathway which tempted him to follow it
toward some holy but unimagined goal.

"There may be, at the first," he wrote,
"a faint flurry of skepticism. But after a
while the whole world will feel certain I
have taken my own life with a most explain-
able motive. . . Adela Atterbury will have
her burst of indignant denial, her sense of
outraged credulity. But with her, as with
Mrs. Westerveldt, there will come in time
an acceptance of the general verdict. Be it
your part never to divulge the truth, and to
destroy these lines within the hour of reading them.

"And now farewell, my friend. Long
years of happiness and health to you and
to *her*. You know we never believed in
'visions,' you and I. And yet I seem to
be visited, at this moment, by a vision of
your perfect future joy. Feeling oneself
on the threshold of death, as I feel myself
now, one has the impression of mighty dra-
peries being grasped by some great dusky
hand and lifted upon new yet awful tracts

of shadow. How often have we spoken of death together! You recall that I always told you I had no fear to push my keel out into the icy silence of those waters! Well, the hour of embarkation and of mysterious voyage has begun with me, and I still have no fear—none, not the vaguest qualm. But I am haunted by an irresistible and unforeseen hope. Some might call it a prescience; I have always been wary of those wide-sweeping words. But the chief element of my hope is a longing that I may see your perfect contentment and hers from some unguessed bourne of spiritual vantage. . . My will, as I wrote pages back, was made weeks ago in your favor. There will be no contention of it, since I am quite kinless in so far as I know, and the claim of any remote relative would rightly be judged absurd. Besides, I think, not even such a claimant as that could arise. Strangely enough, I seem to find myself the last survivor of two races. With me both lines melt into extinction. *Non omnis moriar*, let me add. Will not you say 'amen' to that?

Perhaps not now: but some future day shall teach you to speak the words without sorrow, and with moderation, not overplus, of thanks. . .

" After all, there are some superstitions that do us good. Cherish this one:—that in dying I take away her curse. It is pretty, is it not? Cling to it if you can." . . .

*　　　*　　　*　　　*　　　*

In the morning when they knocked at his door there came the silence that made them knock louder, and at length the silence that sanctioned rude entrance.

He lay as if he slept. But his extreme pallor sublimated the beauty of his brow and temples, and clad his pure-carven lips with some delicate mingling of sadness and peace which was like a tangible echo of the word "death."

THE END.

www.ingramcontent.com/pod-product-compliance
Lightning Source LLC
Chambersburg PA
CBHW031406270326
41929CB00010BA/1349